Teacher's Book **2**

Third Edition

# Person to Person

## Communicative Speaking and Listening Skills

D0743756

**Jack C. Richards**     **David Bycina**     **Ingrid Wisniewska**

**Genevieve Kocienda**

OXFORD

UNIVERSITY PRESS

UNIVERSITY PRESS

198 Madison Avenue
New York, NY 10016 USA

Great Clarendon Street, Oxford OX2 6DP UK

Oxford University Press is a department of the University of Oxford.
It furthers the University's objective of excellence in research, scholarship,
and education by publishing worldwide in

Oxford New York

Auckland Cape Town Dar es Salaam Hong Kong Karachi
Kuala Lumpur Madrid Melbourne Mexico City Nairobi
New Delhi Shanghai Taipei Toronto

With offices in

Argentina Austria Brazil Chile Czech Republic France Greece
Guatemala Hungary Italy Japan Poland Portugal Singapore
South Korea Switzerland Thailand Turkey Ukraine Vietnam

OXFORD and OXFORD ENGLISH are registered trademarks of
Oxford University Press

Executive Publisher: Nancy Leonhardt
Senior Acquisitions Editor: Chris Balderston
Senior Editor: Patricia O'Neill
Associate Editor: Amy E. Hawley
Assistant Editor: Kate Schubert
Art Director: Maj-Britt Hagsted
Layout Artist: Elsa Varela
Art Editor: Robin Fadool
Production Manager: Shanta Persaud
Production Controller: Eve Wong

ISBN-13: 978 0 19 430220 3
ISBN-10: 0 19 430220 2

Printed in Hong Kong.

Printing (last digit): 10 9 8 7 6 5 4 3 2

ACKNOWLEDGMENTS

*Optional Activities* written by Michelle Johnstone

*Illustrations and realia by*: Karen Minot: 115, 118, 124, 130; Geo Parkin: 125.

*Cover photograph by*: Dennis Kitchen Studio

# Scope and Sequence

## Introduction                                                                 vii

## Unit 1                                                                   page 2

**Functions**

Starting a conversation, extending a conversation, asking if you've met before, introducing friends, making small talk

**Topics**

Events, leisure activities, introductions

**Structures**

Tag questions, Yes/No questions, short answers and responses, simple past, present perfect, strong adjectives

**Pronunciation Focus**

Rising and falling intonation

## Unit 2                                                                  page 10

**Functions**

Asking where services are located, describing buildings, asking for directions in a store, asking for directions in a mall

**Topics**

Directions, buildings, errands, accessories

**Structures**

*Where can I...?*, requests with embedded questions, prepositions of place, place expressions

**Pronunciation Focus**

Consonant clusters

## Unit 3                                                                  page 18

**Functions**

Asking to speak to someone, offering to take a message, taking a message, calling for information, asking for additional information, leaving a message

**Topics**

Talking on the telephone, getting information over the phone

**Structures**

Requests with *could*, use of *will* for offers

**Pronunciation Focus**

Stress placement on multisyllabic words

## Review: Units 1–3                                                       page 26

## Unit 4                                                                  page 28

**Functions**

Identifying a problem, making suggestions, asking for and giving advice, describing consequences

**Topics**

Public and private issues, solutions, and consequences

**Structures**

Modal verbs *can*, *would*, *should*, conditionals, *Why don't...?*

**Pronunciation Focus**

Intonation in Wh-questions and Yes/No questions

## Unit 5 — page 36

**Functions**
Asking about other people, reacting to good and bad news, asking for more details, saying what someone should have done, interrupting and getting back to the story

**Topics**
Life events and problems

**Structures**
Present perfect, simple past, past continuous, future with *be going to*, *should* + perfect infinitive (*should have done*), adverbs of time and manner, strong adjectives

**Pronunciation Focus**
Stressed and unstressed words in sentences

## Unit 6 — page 44

**Functions**
Talking about symptoms, giving, accepting, and refusing advice, advising someone *not* to do something, asking for advice, giving and asking about instructions

**Topics**
Illnesses, remedies, prescriptions

**Structures**
Modal verbs *should*, *'d better*, *must*, *could*, *can't*

**Pronunciation Focus**
Unstressed prepositions

## Review: Units 4–6 — page 52

## Unit 7 — page 54

**Functions**
Describing what objects are used for, giving instructions, discussing needs and requirements, asking for clarification, talking about consequences

**Topics**
Kitchen utensils, recipes, outdoor activities and equipment

**Structures**
*Used/be for* + gerund, *used/be to* + base form, sequence adverbs, imperative (with *you*)

**Pronunciation Focus**
Blending of final [t] of a word with initial consonant of next word

## Unit 8 — page 62

**Functions**
Asking about types of hotels, asking for details, making a reservation, checking in, making requests, asking about hotel services

**Topics**
Hotels, reservations, services

**Structures**
Requests, Yes/No questions, embedded questions

**Pronunciation Focus**
Unstressed form of *can*

## Unit 9 — page 70

**Functions**
Getting information, discussing possible activities, asking about public transportation, talking about tours

**Topics**
Travel, sight-seeing itineraries, tourist activities, using public transportation, guided tours

**Structures**
Review of *should* and *can*, conditionals

**Pronunciation Focus**
Linking of final [t] sound to initial vowel sound of next word

## Review: Units 7–9 · page 78

## Unit 10 · page 80

| Functions | Topics | Structures | Pronunciation Focus |
|---|---|---|---|
| Asking who someone is, identifying someone, asking what someone is like, discussing qualities | Personal descriptions, positive and negative characteristics | Relative clauses, adjectives for personal description, modifiers | [r] sound after a vowel |

## Unit 11 · page 88

| Functions | Topics | Structures | Pronunciation Focus |
|---|---|---|---|
| Discussing experiences, telling a story, responding to someone's story | Hobbies, leisure activities, reactions, past experiences | Present perfect, simple past, past continuous, time clauses with *when* | Past-tense ending *-ed* |

## Unit 12 · page 96

| Functions | Topics | Structures | Pronunciation Focus |
|---|---|---|---|
| Asking and giving opinions, agreeing and disagreeing with opinions, giving reasons, social issues, seeing the other side | Movies, TV shows, books | Simple past, *neither/so*, *too/either*, negative Wh-questions | Soft and hard [th] sounds |

## Review: Units 10–12 · page 104

## Optional Activities · page 106

# Introduction

## New to this edition

**Student CD**
A Student CD is included in the back of the Student Book to provide students with listening practice outside of class.

**Consider This**
Each unit opens with a Consider This activity. It provides cross-cultural input and serves as a quick introduction to the unit.

**Use These Words**
This new feature provides vocabulary support for students as they complete the Practice activities.

**Now Try This**
This addition to the Person to Person pages offers extension activities that can be done as a class or by students who finish earlier than their classmates.

**Test Booklet**
The completely revised test program now provides photocopiable tests for all 12 units of the Student Book to assess both listening and speaking. There is an audio CD in the back of the booklet containing the listening material. Answer keys and the audio script are also included.

## Components

*Person to Person*, Third Edition, Book 2 consists of:

### • Student Book with CD

The Student Book contains 12 units, each unit made up of two lessons. Each lesson contains: a Conversation, Give It a Try, and Listen to This. The Let's Talk activity in the first lesson allows students to practice the functions of the lesson in a less controlled activity. Each unit ends with Person to Person, which gives students an opportunity to work together on task-based communicative activities using the functions taught in the unit. The types of practice range from controlled to free use of the language. Review units after every third unit also consolidate the functions from those units. The Student CD in the back of the book contains Conversations 1 and 2 from each lesson, and can be used by students outside of class for additional listening practice.

### • Audio CDs

*Person to Person*, Third Edition, provides many opportunities to listen to native and non-native speakers. The Class CDs have recordings for:

1. *Conversation.* The conversation that opens each lesson in the unit is presented at a normal, natural speed. Accompanying comprehension questions and answers are provided in the Teacher's Book.

2. *Give It a Try.* Sample dialogue based on the text presented in the function boxes are now recorded to provide students with more listening examples.

3. *Listen to This.* This listening selection includes conversations that will help students perform real-life listening tasks such as finding out about opening and closing times, getting directions, and listening to and writing down information on forms.

4. *Pronunciation Focus.* The examples in the Pronunciation Focus are now included on the CD to further enhance pronunciation practice.

The audio script is at the back of the Student Book. It should not be referred to unless necessary after students have heard a recording several times.

Recorded material is identified by this icon 💿 , which includes the audio track number for easy reference.

### • Teacher's Book

The Teacher's Book presents step-by-step procedures for teaching each unit. Notes on language, culture, and pronunciation are provided throughout in anticipation of areas that may cause difficulty for students. Optional Activities, which may be photocopied for students, are also provided for each unit. The entire audio script of the Student Book is included in the Teacher's Book.

### • Test Booklet

The test package has been completely revised for the third edition. The Test Booklet contains photocopiable tests for each unit in the Student Book, as well as an answer key and audio script. The audio CD in the back of the booklet contains recordings for all of the listening sections of the tests.

## A Communicative Approach

Over the years, there has been a de-emphasis on grammatical competence as the primary goal of language learning and a focus on communicative objectives instead. This has resulted in less attention to the rules of English grammar and grammatical accuracy, and more interest in the processes of communication and conversational fluency as a goal in conversation classes. For this reason, the focus of each unit in *Person to Person* is not on grammar, but on conversational tasks or functions, such as talking about likes and dislikes, or asking permission.

Although grammatical competence is a component of conversational proficiency, there are additional skills specific to conversation. Some of the most important of these skills and abilities are discussed below.

## Topics

To be able to converse, the learner must be familiar with a broad range of common topics that occur in everyday conversation. He or she needs to be able to respond to and initiate questions on the situations, events, and activities that are commonly referred to during social interaction with speakers of English. This means having sufficient vocabulary not only to be able to recognize what was said, but also to have something to say or add in response.

## Speech Functions

When people meet they do more than exchange information. They use language to make social interaction possible. This involves the ability to carry out different kinds of conversational tasks and speech functions, such as to greet and acknowledge people, to open and close conversations comfortably, and to introduce and develop topics naturally. When we speak to people we not only *say* things, we *do* things: we describe events and feelings, make requests, and offer suggestions and recommendations, as well as respond and react to suggestions, requests, orders, and so on. These are the speech functions we use for conversation and which learners of English need to practice.

To illustrate the importance of language functions, let's take the example *will*. In grammar classes students learn that *will* has future meaning. However, *will* covers a variety of functions: prediction (*I think it will rain tomorrow.*), warning (*Be careful or you'll fall.*), offer (*I'll do it.*), request (*Will you open the door?*), threat (*Do that again and I'll scream!*), and promise (*I'll take you out for dinner if you pass the test.*). If students aren't aware of these uses of *will*, they are likely to think that *will* is interchangeable with other future forms, resulting in inappropriate utterances. For example, they need to understand that *Are you going to open the door?* is not equivalent to *Will you open the door?* And the answer to *What are you doing after work?* cannot be *I'll go home.*

Just as a single structure can be used to express a number of functions, so can a given function be communicated by a range of grammatical forms. Consider how many ways advice can be given. We can use modals (*Maybe you should/ought to lie down.*), questions (*Why don't you lie down?* or *Have you thought about lying down?*), or the conditional (*If I were you, I would lie down.*). In order to develop the necessary conversational and listening skills, extensive practice is needed, and this is what *Person to Person* provides.

## Unpredictable Forms

When we perform different kinds of speech functions, we usually take part in a series of exchanges. For example, I *invite* you to a movie. You *accept* the invitation and *inquire* where and when we will meet. I *suggest* a time and a place. You *accept* my suggestion or *suggest* an alternative. But although this sequence of functions can be predicted once the function of the first utterance in the series is determined, the *actual words and phrases used* to express each function cannot be predicted. Conversational competence requires the listener to match and understand the meanings of different sentences and phrases according to where they occur within an exchange.

## Appropriate Language

The degree of social distance between speakers influences the forms of address used, what is talked about, and how it is said. For each interaction, a speaker must decide what the relationship between the speaker and hearer is, then adjust his/her conversational choices accordingly. Thus, in speaking to a professor a student may ask, *Could I possibly speak with you for a minute?* and to a friend, *Hey, Bob, got a minute?*

As well as using language that is sufficiently polite or casual for the situation, we must also express speech functions according to the conventions of English. We can greet a person in English with *How are you?*, but although the expressions *Are you well?* and *How is your health?* are both English, they are not customarily used as greetings. A great deal of conversational language is, in this sense, idiomatic and conventional.

## Mutually Created

Conversation is a two-way process. Participants share the responsibility of maintaining the flow of talk and making their contributions both comprehensible and relevant. Conversational competence thus involves the integration of grammatical skills with the other skills noted above, and practice in this is what *Person to Person* provides.

The functions and topics included in *Person to Person* are based on a consideration of communicative needs and related grammar skills required of students at the basic and intermediate levels. A complete list of the functions and topics appears in the Scope and Sequence on pages iii–v.

## How a Lesson Works

### Consider This

The first page of each unit contains a Consider This section. These contain factual information related to the topic of the unit. They can be used as a warm-up to the unit, and are intended to introduce cross-cultural information into the lesson.

Time: approximately 5 minutes

## Conversation

Each unit has two lessons. Each lesson begins with a recorded conversation that includes examples of the functions to be studied in that lesson. Two subsections— Prelistening Questions and Vocabulary—can help prepare students to listen the conversation.

### Prelistening Questions

These questions are designed to stimulate students' interest and focus them on the topic of the conversation. Discussing the questions either in pairs, small groups, or as a class enables students to better make use of their knowledge of the topic as they listen to the conversation.

### Vocabulary

The Teacher's Book suggests vocabulary items for presentation with each conversation. It is up to you to choose if and when to introduce them. You may wish to postpone the introduction of new vocabulary until after the students have heard the conversation once. This will encourage them to get the message from the whole conversation, rather than listen for individual words. Thus, students learn to keep listening even if they hear a word or two they don't understand.

When appropriate, provide a picture or example of the item being introduced. Alternatively, write the word on the board and present the definition given in the Teacher's Book. If time permits, ask students to make an original sentence with each new item. You may also wish to simply translate the word or expression, or allow the students to use a bilingual dictionary. In most instances, students will benefit more from using the context to understand the meaning.

### Listening

Students should have several opportunities to hear the conversation. First, play the entire conversation without stopping. Then, play it again with frequent pauses during which students can repeat the lines. They will also read it afterward. As they do so, have them practice the "read and look up" technique:

One student looks at the text to be read aloud. When ready to speak, he or she looks at his or her partner and says a line (or part of a line). He or she then looks down at the page again for the next line, and again looks up while saying it. The reader's eyes should never be in the book while he or she is speaking. This will help students to role-play more naturally. At the same time, it will improve their reading fluency by requiring them to take in phrases, rather than read word-by-word. Although students may resist this technique in the beginning, repeated practice will help them see how useful it is.

Time: approximately 20 minutes

## Give It a Try

Every function heard in the conversation is presented separately in the Give It a Try section. This allows each function to be concentrated on individually. Follow the suggestions in the Teacher's Book for teaching pronunciation points where applicable. Notes on culture, grammar, and usage are also provided to enable you to present the functions more effectively. The guided Practice activities give each learner an opportunity to practice the new functions with a partner or in a small group. They include practice with content in the Student Book and provide opportunities for students to use the same functions to practice talking about their own ideas and experiences.

Time: approximately 15 minutes for each numbered subsection

## Use These Words

The "Use These Words" feature is new in this third edition. It occurs once per lesson in the Give It a Try sections, and provides vocabulary support by giving students access to words they can use to do the Practice activities. You can draw students' attention to this as you see fit. As an extension activity, ask students to add to the list by thinking of their own ideas or using their dictionaries for help.

## Listen to This

Both lessons in each unit have a task-based listening section called Listen to This, which is designed to help students with real-life listening tasks. Following a presentation of the recording, students listen again to check their own answers before comparing with partners or with the class. Each Listen to This section in the Teacher's Book contains the audioscript and an answer key along with a suggested teaching procedure for that section.

Time: approximately 20 minutes

## Let's Talk

Each unit has a speaking activity, Let's Talk, which is presented at the end of the first lesson. It provides an opportunity to practice the functions and vocabulary of the first lesson in a less-controlled activity, and prepares students for the Person to Person activity at the end of the unit.

Time: approximately 15–20 minutes

## Person to Person

At the end of each unit, partners work together on a communicative task-based activity based on the functions in the unit. Each partner has information that the other needs to complete the activity, so it is necessary to give and receive information carefully. Students are separated into pairs, and each student reads the information for his or her part according to the instructions in the Student Book.

Expressing personal opinions and ideas, along with active listening, is an important part of this section.

Time: approximately 20–30 minutes

### Now Try This

New in this third edition, Now Try This is an extension activity for the Person to Person activity. It can be done by students who finish earlier than their classmates, or it can be done by the whole class to finish off the lesson.

Time: approximately 5 minutes

## Optional Activities

Two optional photocopiable activities are provided for each unit. Suggested teaching procedures and answers appear in the back of the Teacher's Book. You should allow for time constraints, student progress, or other pedagogical considerations when presenting them. It is necessary to make copies of the Optional Activity for each student before class.

Time: approximately 15–25 minutes

## Review Units

There are four Review Units in the Student Book. The first covers Units 1–3, the second covers the next three units, and so on. Each Review provides students an opportunity to practice the functions through a listening and speaking activity for each unit.

Time: approximately 15–25 minutes per unit

# Additional Considerations

## Grammar and Usage

*Person to Person* is not meant to be a grammar text. The authors assume that basic grammar has already been learned and that here the students need practice in using grammar in a natural, conversational setting. However, please note that grammar is carefully controlled so that, as far as possible, the major points of English grammar are reviewed in natural contexts. The units progress in grammatical difficulty, although they can be done out of sequence if the class can handle it. Language Notes, usually found in the Give it a Try sections, contain important grammar and usage explanations. A summary of the grammar points in each unit of the Student Book appears in the Scope and Sequence Chart on pages iii–v.

## Pronunciation

Each unit highlights one pronunciation point in the Pronunciation Focus. In addition, other pronunciation points are highlighted in the Teacher's Book. By paying particular attention to these pronunciation points, you will give your students an awareness of those features of American English that will be most useful to them as both listeners and speakers. These pronunciation points are:

sentence stress, intonation, rhythm, blending, and reduction.

### Sentence stress and intonation

Speakers use stress and intonation to mark the words they want to highlight, to signal the end of a thought unit, and to indicate such things as whether that unit is part of a series or a completed thought, whether it is a statement, a *Wh-* question, a Yes/No question, or a request.

## Intonation Patterns

Speakers of English use various intonation patterns when conversing with others. Here are some examples:

request: Could I have your name, please?

statement: It's Paine.

*Wh-* question: How do you spell that?

series: It's P-a-i-n-e.

Yes/No question: Do you live in Chicago?

### Blending and reduction

Words that are not given strong stress are often said quickly, "swallowed," or otherwise altered. *What did he* becomes /wuh-de/, *could you* becomes /cu-juh/, *did she* becomes /che/, and so on. This is because English is a stress-timed language. In contrast to many languages where speaking each syllable takes the same length of time, English requires *only* those syllables that are stressed to be said slowly. When listening to a rapid stream of speech, students of English sometimes find it hard to recognize even words that they know because they are unfamiliar with their unstressed (or reduced) forms. Part of communicative competence, then, is to be able to recognize reduced forms as well as grasp how stress is used communicatively, such as to highlight important ideas. *Person to Person* addresses these features of pronunciation throughout the Teacher's Book.

General considerations for teaching:

- To heighten students' awareness of the stress, tap out the rhythm or clap your hands, hitting the stressed syllables with greater force. This will also help students see that the rhythm is very even, which is why words get reduced.
- On the board, write intonation and stress patterns with examples.
- Emphasize the pronunciation point as you model the examples given in the Teacher's Book.
- Try to integrate pronunciation work with activities whenever possible. This will help students grasp that control of pronunciation is an essential part of communicative competence. However, during guided practice or role plays it is vital that students be encouraged to develop their fluency and not be interrupted. Pronunciation work should be done either during presentation of a conversation or function, or after the students have completed pair or group work.

## Pair Work

*Person to Person* is based on pair and small-group activities that maximize each student's opportunity to speak in class. Clear language models and guided activities enable pairs to work alone effectively. The elements of real communication are simulated in role plays and information-gap activities. While practicing, it is important to remind students that communication is much more than words. People say a lot with their faces, their gestures, and their tone of voice.

As students practice in pairs or small groups, you can walk around the room and listen to them. In many instances, you will hear incorrect usage, hesitancy, unclear pronunciation, and other areas you may want to work on. It is important, however, not to interrupt the students during free practice. Note the areas that need work and assist the students afterward. Establish yourself as a resource. Encourage students to call on you when they need help.

The procedures mentioned throughout the Teacher's Book are only suggestions. Adapt them in accordance with your own preferences and the particular needs of your students. You will need to experiment to find what works best for your class, keeping in mind that extensive pair work will maximize class time.

# Haven't we met before?

## Components

Student Book, pages 2–9, 106
Class CD 1, Tracks 2–12
Optional Activities 1.1–1.2,
page 106

## Objectives

**Functions:** Starting a conversation, extending a conversation, asking if you've met before, introducing friends, making small talk

**Topics:** Events, leisure activities, introductions

**Structures:** Tag questions, Yes/No questions, short answers and responses, simple past, present perfect, strong adjectives

**Pronunciation Focus:** Rising and falling intonation

**Listen to This:** Listening for gist: situations, topics; listening for specific information: names, places; making inferences: relationships, level of formality; matching conversations to expressions, filling in charts

---

**Student Book page 2**

## CONSIDER THIS

1. Have students read the information and the questions. Go over vocabulary students don't know.

2. Group Work. Divide students into groups of four or five. Have students in each group take turns asking and answering the questions. Help with vocabulary as needed.

3. Ask volunteers to give their answers to the questions.

4. If time allows, discuss greetings in the students' country. Are they always the same or is the greeting different depending on gender, age, situation, or social position?

## Vocabulary

Introduce these phrases to the students:

*film festival:* a group of related films shown during a specific time period at a particular place

*to look familiar:* to seem that another person has seen or met you before

*at first:* in the beginning

## Prelistening

1. Pair Work. Have students open their books and look at the photograph. Have partners describe what they see to each other. Circulate and help with vocabulary as needed.

2. Class Work. Read the title of the conversation and the prelistening question and task. Ask volunteers to answer the question.

3. Pair Work. Have students list places where they can make friends with English speakers.

4. Class Work. Have pairs read their lists to the class. Make a master list on the board.

## Conversation 1

**Class CD 1, Track 2**

1. With books closed, play the recording or read the conversation.

Pete: This is a great film festival, isn't it?
Liz: It sure is. This film looks wonderful.
Pete: Yes, it does. Have you been to this film festival before?
Liz: Yes, I was here last year.
Pete: This is my first time. You know, you look familiar. Haven't we met before?
Liz: I'm not sure.
Pete: I think we were in the same computer class last year. With Ms. Clark?
Liz: I remember you now!
Pete: My name's Pete. Pete Wilson.
Liz: I'm·Liz Wu. It's good to see you again. Sorry I didn't recognize you at first.
Pete: Well, my hair was a lot longer then, and I wore glasses.

2. Ask these comprehension questions:

• *Where are they?* (in a movie theater)
• *What is the event?* (a film festival)

- *What's the woman's name?* (Liz Wu)
- *What's the man's name?* (Pete Wilson)

3. Play or read the conversation again, pausing for choral repetition.

4. Ask the following questions:
   - *Is Speaker 1 enjoying the film festival?* (yes)
   - *Has Speaker 2 been to the film festival before?* (yes, last year)
   - *Where do they know each other from?* (a computer class)
   - *How has Speaker 1 changed?* (He had longer hair and glasses.)

   Elicit responses from various students.

5. Paired Reading. Have students read the conversation, switching roles.

**Student Book page 3**

## Give It a Try

### 1. Conversational openings

Review. Ask students to greet each other. Move rapidly around the classroom.

#### *Presentation*

1. Have students look at the function box. Give them time to read the examples.

2. Model the exchanges and have students repeat chorally.

3. Practice a few exchanges with various students.

#### Notes

1. On the board, write the following statements and mark the stress and intonation:

   *This film looks <u>wonderful</u>.*

   *It <u>sure</u> does.*

   Emphasize the stress placement on the words that show how the speakers feel (*great, sure*) as you model the examples.

2. Point out that speakers often talk about the immediate environment when they begin a conversation with a stranger in a public place or at a party.

#### *Practice 1*

**Class CD 1, Track 3**

1. Have students read the directions and the lists of openings and responses.

2. Play or read the example conversation twice.

   A: This is a great film festival, isn't it?
   B: It sure is. This film looks wonderful.
   A: It sure does.

3. Pair Work. Have students take turns beginning a conversation using the openings and responses listed.

4. Ask several pairs to demonstrate for the class.

#### *Practice 2*

1. Have students read the directions and look at the words in the box. Explain any words students don't know.

2. Give students time to think of conversational openings for each situation. If necessary, brainstorm possible openings and responses with the class.

3. Pair Work. Have students take turns opening a conversation and responding for each of the situations.

4. Have several pairs demonstrate for the class.

### 2. Extending the conversation

#### *Presentation*

1. Have students look at the function boxes. Give them time to read the examples.

2. Model the exchanges and have students repeat chorally.

3. Pair Work. Have several pairs model the exchanges with different combinations.

#### Note

Explain to students that when talking to a stranger at a party, it is best not to ask any personal questions, but to keep to questions about the party.

#### *Practice*

**Class CD 1, Track 4**

1. Have students read the directions.

2. Play or read the example conversation twice.

   A: This is a great film festival, isn't it?
   B: It sure is. The films are wonderful.
   A: Have you been to this film festival before?
   B: Yes, I was here last year.

3. Divide the class into new pairs. Give students time to think of conversational openings, responses, and questions to extend the conversation for each situation. If necessary, brainstorm ideas with the class.

4. Pair Work. Have students take turns opening and extending the conversation in the situations on the list.

5. Ask several pairs to demonstrate for the class.

## Extension

1. Divide the class into groups of four. Have groups think of two more situations and conversations and then demonstrate them for the class in pairs. Make sure that students are asking and answering questions appropriately and not being too personal.

2. Have students use their dictionaries to add words to the **Use These Words** list.

**Student Book page 4**

# 3. Asking if you've met before

## Presentation

1. Have students look at the function box. Give them time to read the examples.

2. Model the exchanges and have students repeat chorally.

3. Practice a few exchanges with various students.

### Notes

1. Review tag question pronunciation. On the board, write the following question:

   *You were in my computer class, weren't you?*

   Point out that, in tag questions, rising intonation implies that the speaker is not sure of the answer and falling intonation implies that the speaker is more certain of the answer. Model the two ways of pronouncing the tag question and have students repeat.

2. Point out that *You were in my computer class, weren't you?* and *Weren't you in my computer class?* have the same meaning, but the latter is more often used when the speaker is not sure of the answer.

## Practice 1

**Class CD 1, Track 5**

1. Have students read the directions and the list. Give students time to add their own idea to the list.

2. Play or read the example conversation twice.

   A: Don't I know you from somewhere?
   B: I'm not sure. Do you?
   A: I think we met at Sam's birthday party.
   B: Oh, yes. I remember you now.
   A: My name's Pete. Pete Wilson.
   B: I'm Liz Wu.

3. Divide students into pairs.

4. Pair Work. Have students take turns asking if they have met before. Make sure they use affirmative and negative answers.

5. Ask several pairs to demonstrate for the class.

## Practice 2

1. Have students read the directions.

2. Give students time to think of situations where they could have met someone. Encourage them to use their imagination.

3. Have students circulate around the class and ask each other if they have met before.

4. Have several pairs demonstrate for the class.

## Extension

Have the class vote on the most imaginative or funniest situation.

## Listen to This

**Class CD 1, Track 6**

**Part 1**

1. Have students read the directions and look at the places listed. Explain what a reunion is, if necessary.

2. Play or read the conversations. Tell students to write the number of each conversation next to the matching location on the list.

   **1**
   M: There are a lot of people in this class, aren't there?
   L: Yes, I didn't know it would be so crowded.
   M: Do you mind if I share your book just for today's class? I haven't bought mine yet.
   L: Sure. No problem. Haven't we met somewhere before?
   M: I'm not sure.... Were you in Mrs. Brown's English class last semester?
   L: No, I wasn't. I took French last semester. Maybe we met at registration or something.
   M: Yes! That was it! You were next to me in the line for registration last week.
   L: Nice to see you again! My name's Lee.
   M: I'm Mike.

   **2**
   R: This food looks really delicious!
   E: Yes, it does. The bride looks so happy, too.
   R: Are you a friend of Janet's?
   E: Yes, I am. We went to high school together. How about you?
   R: I'm a friend of hers too, from college. But I have the feeling we've met before somewhere....
   E: Have we? Were you at Janet's twenty-first birthday party?
   R: Yes, I was! I remember now, you were sitting at the other end of the table.
   E: Yes, nice to meet you finally! I'm Eve.
   R: Nice to meet you, too. My name's Ruth.

**3**

S: There are so many people here, but no one that I really recognize. Have you seen anyone you know yet? Wait a minute.... Aren't you Joe Simpson?

J: Yes, I am.

S: I'm Stan MacDonald. We were on the soccer team together, remember?

J: Yes, that's right! Good to see you again, Stan.

S: It's good to see you, too. You haven't changed a bit!

J: I don't play much now though. Did you see that match between England and Brazil?

3. Play or read the conversations again for students to check their answers.

4. Ask volunteers for their answers.

> **Answers:**
> 1. in a class
> 2. at a friend's wedding
> 3. at a high school reunion

### Part 2

1. Have students read the directions and look at the chart.

2. Play or read the conversations again and have students fill in the information on the chart. Students may need to hear the conversations again to get all the information. Pause after each conversation, if needed.

3. Play or read the conversations again for students to check their answers.

4. Ask volunteers for their answers.

> **Answers:**
> 1. Lee and Mike; in the line for registration
> 2. Eve and Ruth; at Janet's twenty-first birthday party
> 3. Joe Simpson and Stan MacDonald; on the soccer team

### Part 3

1. Have students read the directions.

2. Play or read the first sentence of each conversation. Write them on the board, if necessary.

3. Group Work. Divide the class into groups of four or five and have them think of other conversational openings for each situation.

4. Ask volunteers to report their discussion to the class.

## Let's Talk

### Part 1

1. Have students read the directions and write three sentences about events or places they have been to. Tell them they can write true or untrue statements.

2. Circulate and help as needed.

### Note

If you have a high-level class, tell students to think of at least one unusual thing that is not true, but believable, but not to tell anyone which event or place it is. At the end of Part 3, have students guess which one of the three things was not true for each student.

### Part 2

1. Have students read the directions.

2. Model the activity. Write a place or event on a piece of paper. Walk up to a student, exchange your papers, and say: *We are at the park with our dogs.* Have the student open the conversation. Extend the conversation with the student with one or two exchanges. Then have the student look at your piece of paper and ask if you have met before at that place or event.

3. Tell students to stand up and walk around the classroom. Say *Stop* and tell students to pair with the student closest to them. Tell them they are on a golf course, at a bookstore, or some other place or event.

4. Have students follow the model and have their own conversation until you tell them to stop talking.

### Part 3

1. Have students read the directions.

2. Ask various students to report on what they learned about their classmates.

# I've heard a lot about you.

## Vocabulary

Introduce these words and phrases to the students:

*amazing*: wonderful, fantastic

*jam session*: a meeting of musicians to play music together, usually improvising

*sounds cool*: an informal way to say that something sounds fun and/or interesting

## Prelistening

1. Have students open their books and look at the photograph. Ask:

   • *Where are they?* (in a cafe)
   • *Do the three people already know each other?* (No, two of the people are meeting for the first time.)

2. Read the title of the conversation and the prelistening question and task.

3. Pair Work. Divide the class into pairs. Have pairs make lists of topics you talk about when you meet someone for the first time.

4. Class Work. Have pairs share their lists with the class. Make a master list on the board.

## Conversation 2

**Class CD 1, Track 7**

1. With books closed, play the recording or read the conversation.

   | | |
   |---|---|
   | Luis: | Hey. Sorry I'm late. |
   | Liz: | That's OK. We just got here. Luis, this is my friend Eun-joo. Eun-joo, this is Luis. We met in class last year. |
   | Eun-joo: | Hi, Luis. Nice to meet you. |
   | Luis: | Hi, Eun-joo. I've heard a lot about you. |
   | Liz: | Luis just got back from Hong Kong. |
   | Eun-joo: | Really? How was it? |
   | Luis: | It was amazing. |
   | Liz: | You went to a rock concert there, didn't you? |
   | Luis: | Yeah, my friends are in a band, so they gave me free tickets. |
   | Eun-joo: | I hear you're a good bass player. |
   | Luis: | I'm not bad. But I haven't played that much recently. Do you play music? |
   | Eun-joo: | Yes, I do. Actually, my friends are having a jam session this weekend. Do you want to come? |
   | Luis: | Sounds cool! |

2. Ask these comprehension questions:

   • *Where did Speaker 2 meet Speaker 3?* (in class last year)
   • *Where did Speaker 1 just come back from?* (Hong Kong)

3. Say: *Listen again. This time listen for the details of the conversation.*

4. Play or read the conversation again, pausing for choral repetition. Allow students to write down the information as they listen. Play or read the conversation again, if needed, for students to get all the information.

5. Ask the following questions:

   • *What did Speaker 1 do in Hong Kong?* (He went to a rock concert.)
   • *Did he pay for the tickets?* (No, his friends in the band gave them to him.)
   • *What instrument does Speaker 1 play?* (the bass)
   • *Has he played a lot recently?* (no)
   • *Does Speaker 3 play music?* (yes)
   • *When is the jam session?* (this weekend)

   Elicit responses from various students.

## Note

In the United States, work is a common subject of first conversations because it is considered neutral and uncontroversial. Topics that are inappropriate for a first conversation include: personal problems, negative news, money, or anything that elicits strong opinions.

## PRONUNCIATION FOCUS

**Class CD 1, Track 8**

1. Explain what the focus is. Play or read the examples in the book and have students repeat chorally.

   **Luis, this is my friend Eun-joo.**
   **Eun-joo, this is Luis.**

2. With books open, play or read the conversation again. Tell students to pay attention to the intonation.

3. Paired Reading. Have students practice the conversation, switching roles.

## Extension

Write Conversation 2 on the board, leaving out several key words. Tell students to close their books and to write the missing words in their notebooks. Vary the activity by leaving out all the prepositions, all the information words, or all the nouns or verbs.

**Student Book page 7**

## Give It a Try

Review. Name a place or situation such as "at the library," "in line at the movie theater," etc. Point to a student and have him or her open a conversation with the student next to him or her. Have that student respond. Move rapidly around the classroom.

## 1. Introducing friends

### Presentation

1. Have students look at the function box. Give them time to read the examples.

2. Model the exchanges and have students repeat chorally.

3. Have groups of three students model some exchanges with different combinations.

### Notes

1. In introductions, stress is placed on the names of the people being introduced. Write the following sentence on the board and mark the stressed words:

   *Eun-joo, this is Luis.*

2. In the United States, when people are introduced in an informal social situation, the first and last or just the first name is used in the introduction. In a more formal or business situation, the first and last names are used. If the person being introduced has a title, such as *Dr.*, that is used as well. In an informal situation, men and women can shake hands or just smile and nod their head. If the other person puts their hand out, it should always be taken. In a formal situation, a handshake is usual for men and women. It is important to make eye contact and have a firm, but not too firm, grip. The person making the introduction should look at and gesture toward the person whose name they are saying at the time.

## Practice

**Class CD 1, Track 9**

1. Have students read the directions.

2. Play or read the example conversation twice.

   A: Luis, this is my friend Eun-joo. Eun-joo, this is Luis. We met in class last year.
   B: Hi, Luis. It's nice to meet you.
   C: Hello, Eun-joo. It's nice to meet you, too.

3. Group Work. Divide students into groups of three. Have students take turns introducing the other people in the group to each other. Make sure they are making eye contact.

4. Have groups demonstrate their conversation for the class.

## 2. Making small talk (1)

### Presentation

1. Have students look at the function box. Give them time to read the examples.

2. Model the exchanges and have students repeat chorally.

3. Have several pairs model the exchanges with different combinations.

### Notes

1. Review intonation of statements and Yes/No questions. On the board, write the following sentences and draw the intonation lines:

   *I hear you like golf.*

   *Do you play golf?*

   *Do you like to play golf?*

   *I love golf.*

   Model the examples and have students repeat.

2. Point out that *Do you* (play music, go jogging, read mysteries)? is used to ask about a person's hobbies.

3. Explain to students that *small talk* is casual non-personal, non-confrontational conversation, usually about unimportant issues.

## Practice

Class CD 1, Track 10

1.  Have students read the directions and look at the pictures and their captions.

2.  Play or read the example conversation.

    A: I hear you're a good bass player.
    B: I'm not bad. Do you play music?
    A: Yes, I do. I play keyboards.
    B: How often do you play?
    A: Every weekend.

3.  Pair Work. Have students take turns making conversation with the words in the captions.

4.  Have various pairs demonstrate for the class.

## Extension

Class Discussion. Discuss with students what people in their country talk about at parties or with strangers in different situations, such as parties, business meetings, at a bus stop, etc.

Student Book page 8

## 3. Making small talk (2)

### Presentation

1.  Have students look at the function box. Give them time to read the examples.

2.  Model the exchanges and have students repeat chorally.

3.  Practice a few exchanges with various students.

### Practice

Class CD 1, Track 11

1.  Have students read the directions and look at the list and the words in the box.

2.  Give students time to write down the four items.

3.  Play or read the example conversation.

    A: Luis, this is my friend Eun-joo.
    B: Hi, Luis, it's nice to meet you.
    C: It's nice to meet you, too.
    A: Luis just got back from Hong Kong.
    B: Really? How was it?
    C: It was amazing.

4.  Group Work. Divide the class into groups of three. Have students exchange their pieces of paper. Then have them take turns introducing each other and asking questions to continue the conversation.

5.  Have several groups demonstrate for the class.

## Extension

1.  Write down conversational openings for various situations, events, and places on slips of paper. Put the slips in a bag or box. Have a student choose one paper and read it to another student. Have that student say something that will continue the conversation. Then have that student choose another paper and continue the process with another student.

2.  Have students use their dictionaries to add words to the **Use These Words** list.

## Listen to This

Class CD 1, Track 12

### Part 1

1.  Give students time to read the directions and look at the chart.

2.  To check comprehension, ask:

    *What will you listen for first?* (the main topic)

    *Where will you write it?* (in the first column)

3.  Play or read the conversations twice. Have students fill in the main topic for each conversation.

    **1**
    S: Hi, Marta! Are you going to the movies with us after class tonight?
    M: Hi, Steve! Sure. I'd love to. By the way, have you met my cousin Tammy? She's visiting us from New York for a few days.
    S: Hi, Tammy. Nice to meet you.
    T: Nice to meet you, too.
    M: Tammy's just seen the latest Johnny Depp movie.
    S: Really? How was it?
    T: Awesome. I love Johnny Depp.

    **2**
    J: Excuse me. Sorry to disturb you. I'd like to introduce Oliver Johnson. He's our marketing consultant in Brazil. He's visiting our offices for a couple of days.
    S: How do you do, Oliver? I'm pleased to meet you. My name's Sam Perez, and I'm the chief financial officer.
    O: I am very glad to meet you.
    J: Oliver has just returned from a trip to Japan to research marketing strategies over there.
    S: Was it interesting?
    O: Yes, fascinating!
    S: I want to hear all about it. Julie, let's have coffee together later on so we can talk more.
    J: Great idea.
    S: See you both later then. Oliver, please enjoy your visit to our offices.
    O: Thank you.

**3**

J: Hi, Max! I haven't seen you in a while!

M: Oh, hi...Janice.

T: (to Janice) I don't think we've met, have we?

M: Oh, uh...Tina, this is Janice, a...friend of mine from high school.

T: Hi, Janice, I'm Tina, Max's girlfriend. Nice to meet you.

J: Max and I are very old friends! How long have you known each other?

T: Not that long. We met on a skiing trip in the Alps last winter.

J: A skiing trip? How romantic! You must be a good skier.

T: I'm not bad. Do you ski?

J: No, I prefer snowboarding.

4. Ask various volunteers for their answers.

> **Answers:**
> 1. movies
> 2. Oliver's trip to Japan
> 3. skiing

**Part 2**

1. Give students time to read the directions.

2. To check comprehension, ask:

   *What will you listen for this time?* (the first names mentioned and relationships)

   *Where will you write it?* (in the second and third columns)

3. Check answers.

> **Answers:**
> 1. Marta, Tammy; cousins
>    Marta, Steve: friends, classmates
> 2. Oliver, Sam, Julie; business colleagues
> 3. Max, Tina; boyfriend and girlfriend
>    Max, Janice: friends

**Part 3**

1. Give students time to read the questions.

2. Pair Work. Have pairs discuss the questions.

3. Ask several pairs to tell their answers.

> **Answers:**
> 1. friendly and informal
> 2. friendly and formal
> 3. unfriendly between Tina and Janice; friendly between Max and Janice

## Person to Person

**Part 1**

1. Divide the class into groups of four and have students decide who will be Student A, Student B, Student C, and Student D. Remind Students C and D to look at page 106.

2. Have students read the directions and look at the information for their character.

3. To check comprehension, ask:

   *Who will you talk to first?* (Students A and B will talk to each other; Students C and D will talk to each other.)

4. Brainstorm with the class appropriate conversational openings for a party for new students.

5. Pair Work. Have pairs role-play the conversations. Circulate and help as needed.

**Part 2**

1. Have students read the directions.

2. To check comprehension, ask:

   *Who will you talk to now?* (Students A, B, C, and D will each introduce their partner to the other three.)

3. Circulate and help students as needed. Make sure students are asking appropriate questions to continue the conversation.

## Now Try This

1. Have students read the directions.

2. Give them time to think of something to say about their partner when introducing him or her.

3. Group Work. Divide the class into new groups of four. Have students take turns introducing their partner to the other two students in the group. Circulate and help as needed.

4. Have groups demonstrate for the class.

## Components

Student Book, pages 10–17, 107
Class CD 1, Tracks 13–23
Optional Activities 2.1–2.2,
page 106

## Objectives

**Functions:** Asking where services are located, describing buildings, asking for directions in a store, asking for directions in a mall

**Topics:** Directions, buildings, errands, accessories

**Structures:** *Where can I...?*, requests with embedded questions, prepositions of place, place expressions

**Pronunciation Focus:** Consonant clusters

**Listen to This:** Listening for specific information: building descriptions and names, locations, floor numbers, store departments, purchase items; locating buildings on a map, filling in a chart

---

**Student Book page 10**

## CONSIDER THIS

1. Have students read the information and the question. Go over vocabulary students don't know.

2. Group Work. Divide students into groups of four or five. Have students discuss where they would like to go shopping—in their country or anywhere else in the world. Help with vocabulary as needed.

3. Ask volunteers for their answers.

### Vocabulary

Introduce these phrases to the students:

*Watch out!*: used to warn someone about something that is just about to happen

*Just my luck!*: used to express the feeling that you are having bad luck, or bad things tend to happen to you

*spare*: an extra one of something

*dry cleaner*: a store that uses a special method to clean clothes that can't be put in a washing machine and usually takes stains out of regular clothes

*dome*: a roof shaped like the half of a sphere

### Prelistening

1. Pair Work. Have students open their books and look at the photograph. Have partners describe what they see to each other. Circulate and help with vocabulary as needed.

2. Class Work. Read the title of the conversation and the prelistening task and questions. Ask volunteers to describe what is happening in the picture and answer the question.

## Conversation 1

**Class CD 1, Track 13**

1. With books closed, play the recording or read the conversation.

Sandy: Watch out! Oh no, you got coffee on your shirt.

Mari: Just my luck! What am I going to do now? I've got my violin recital this afternoon.

Sandy: I could lend you a spare T-shirt if you want.

Mari: Thanks, but I really need this shirt. Do you know where I can get it cleaned? It has to be really fast.

Sandy: Well, I think there's a dry cleaner's in the mall across the street. Or you can try the dry cleaner's on Washington Street. It's next to the King Building.

Mari: OK, I'll try the mall first. Where was the other one?

Sandy: It's a small dry cleaner's next to the King Building on Washington. About two blocks from here.

Mari: Which one is the King Building?

Sandy: It's that big glass office building just past the park. It has a green glass dome on the top.

Mari: OK. Maybe I'll just go buy a new shirt in the mall, what do you think?

Sandy: That might be faster!

2. Ask these comprehension questions:
   - *Where are they?* (in a cafeteria)
   - *What just happened?* (One of the women just spilled coffee on herself.)

3. Play or read the conversation again, pausing for choral repetition.

4. Ask the following questions:
   - *What event does Speaker 2 have to go to?* (a violin recital)
   - *When is the recital?* (this afternoon)
   - *What does Speaker 1 offer to do?* (to lend her a T-shirt)
   - *Does Speaker 2 accept the offer?* (no)
   - *Where are the dry cleaners?* (One is in the mall across the street; the other is on Washington Street next to the King Building.)
   - *What does Speaker 2 decide to do?* (to buy a new shirt in the mall)

   Elicit responses from various students.

5. Paired Reading. Have students read the conversation, switching roles.

**Student Book page 11**

## Give It a Try

## 1. Asking where services are located

Review. Ask students to greet each other. Move rapidly around the classroom.

### Presentation

1. Have students look at the function box. Give them time to read the examples.

2. Model the exchanges and have students repeat chorally.

3. Practice a few exchanges with different combinations with various students.

### Notes

1. In rapid speech, *there's a* is pronounced /therza/. On the board, write the following phrases:

   *There's a dry cleaner...*

   *There's a post office...*

   Model the phrases, emphasizing the blending.

2. Explain the structure

   *get/have* + object + past participle:

   *Where can I have my watched fixed?*

   *Where can I get my hair cut?*

   Explain that the speaker is asking where or how to have a job or service done for them.

3. Explain to students that the expression *to run (an) errand(s)* means to go and take care of tasks such as food shopping, going to the post office, or picking up medicine at the pharmacy.

### Practice 1

**Class CD 1, Track 14**

1. Have students read the directions and look at the list and the map. Go over any vocabulary students don't know.

2. Play or read the example conversation twice.

   A: Excuse me. Where can I get my shirt cleaned?
   B: I think there's a dry cleaner's in the mall across the street.

3. Pair Work. Have students take turns asking where they can run three different errands from the list.

4. Ask several pairs to demonstrate for the class.

### Practice 2

**Class CD 1, Track 15**

1. Have students read the directions and look at the list and the map. Go over any vocabulary students don't know.

2. Play or read the example conversation twice.

   A: Excuse me. Do you know where I can buy a new shirt?
   B: You can try the store on Washington Street. It's next to the King Building.

3. Pair Work. Have students take turns asking where they can run three different errands from the list.

4. Ask several pairs to demonstrate for the class.

### Extension

1. Class Discussion. Discuss with students the kinds of errands they have to run on a daily, weekly, and monthly basis.

2. Write several errands on separate slips of paper and put them in a bag or box. Have a student pick one of the papers and ask another student in the class where he or she can do that errand in the town or city where they live, using either of the example questions from the function box. If the student does not know, then the first student should ask another student until someone can answer the question. Continue the procedure with other students and papers.

## 2. Describing buildings

### Presentation

1. Have students look at the function box. Give them time to read the examples.

2. Model the exchange and have students repeat chorally.

3. Practice a few exchanges with various students.

### Note

Remind students that in noun combinations, the first modifying noun receives stronger stress than the second, as in _police_ station, _department_ store, _reference_ library, or _office_ building.

### Practice

**Class CD 1, Track 16**

1. Have students read the directions and look at the map and the words in the box. Explain any vocabulary students don't know.

2. Play or read the example conversation twice.

   A: Which one is the King Building?
   B: It's the big glass office building just past the park.

3. Pair Work. Have students decide who will be Student A and who will be Student B. Make sure Student A covers the information for Student B.

4. To check comprehension, ask Students B:

   _What does the police station look like?_ (a short red brick building)

   _Where is it located?_ (on Center St. next to the City Reference Library)

5. Have Student A ask Student B to describe three of the buildings on the list. Then have students reverse roles.

6. Ask several pairs to demonstrate for the class.

### Extension

Have students use their dictionaries to add words to the **Use These Words** list.

## Listen to This

**Class CD 1, Track 17**

### Part 1

1. Have students read the directions.

2. Play or read the conversation. Tell students to listen for what Kumiko wants to buy.

   B: Hi, Kumiko. Hey! What's the matter?
   K: It's my boyfriend's birthday tomorrow, and I have no idea what to get him.
   B: No ideas at all?
   K: Well, he needs a new baseball glove. I just went to the Athletic Center, but I couldn't afford the one he really wants. Everything there is way too expensive.
   B: Did you try Sports World?
   K: I've never heard of it.
   B: It's a brand new store, so they're having all sorts of opening week specials. Almost everything is 30 or 40 percent off.
   K: Great. Where is it?
   B: On Duncan Street.
   K: Where is it on Duncan?
   B: Do you know the Manning Building?
   K: Is that the big yellow office building beside the Metro Hotel?
   B: No, that's the Manulife Building. The Manning Building is the tall, glass building across from the hospital. It has a restaurant and observation deck at the top.
   K: OK. I know where it is then.
   B: Sports World is right beside that.
   K: I'll go over there right after lunch. Thanks!
   B: Glad to help. Good luck!

3. Ask volunteers for the answer.

**Answer:**
a new baseball glove

## Part 2

1. Have students read the directions and look at the names of the buildings and the map.

2. Play or read the conversation again and have students write the letter of the building next to the correct name. Students may need to hear the conversations again to get all the information. Pause after the information about each building, if needed.

3. Play or read the conversation again for students to check their answers.

4. Ask volunteers for their answers.

**Answers:**

| | |
|---|---|
| Metro Hotel | C |
| Sports World | B |
| Manning Building | A |
| Manulife Building | D |

## Part 3

1. Have students read the directions.

2. Pair Work. Have partners take turns describing the location of each building and saying what they can do or find in each building.

3. Ask volunteers to describe the location of each building and say what they think is in each building. Make a master list on the board and go over any vocabulary students don't know.

**Possible Answers:**

| | |
|---|---|
| Metro Hotel: | they can stay there |
| Sports World: | they can buy sports equipment and clothing |
| Manning Building: | they can eat at the restaurant there and observe the city from its top |
| Manulife Building: | they can work or go to an office there |

## Let's Talk

### Part 1

1. Have students read the directions and look at the pictures.

2. To check comprehension, ask: *What service does the first picture represent?* (dry cleaning) Continue with the rest of the pictures.

3. Have students write one of the services above the chart.

### Part 2

1. Have students read the directions and look at the chart.

2. Model the activity. Ask a student:

   *Where do you get your clothes dry cleaned? Where is it? What does the building look like?*

3. Tell students to stand up and walk around the classroom. Have them ask ten students where they get that particular service done and ask them questions to fill in the rest of the chart.

4. Circulate and help as needed.

### Part 3

1. Have students read the directions.

2. Have students present their results to the class.

3. Make a master list on the board with the names of the places mentioned for each service. Have students identify the most popular place.

### *Extension*

Brainstorm with students other buildings in their town or city. Ask students to say what they do in that building, what it looks like, and where its located. Have a class vote on what is the most popular (restaurant, museum, coffee shop, etc).

# Where can I find a clothing store?

**Student Book page 14**

## Vocabulary

Introduce these words and phrases to the students:

*several:* more than *a few* but less than *many*

*level:* floor

*hairdresser:* a person who cuts and styles hair

*escalator:* stairs that move by themselves by means of a motor

*flight:* one set of stairs

## Prelistening

1. Have students open their books and look at the photograph. Ask:

   - *Where are they?* (at an information counter in a mall)
   - *Why is the young woman there?* (to buy a new shirt)

2. Pair Work. Read the title of the conversation and the prelistening question and task. Have pairs make lists of reasons why people like or dislike shopping malls.

3. Class Work. Have pairs share their lists with the class. Make a master list on the board.

## Conversation 2

**Class CD 1, Track 18**

1. With books closed, play the recording or read the conversation.

   | | |
   |---|---|
   | Clerk: | Could I help you? |
   | Mari: | Yes, could you tell me where I can find a women's clothing store? |
   | Clerk: | There are several women's clothing stores in the mall. There's one on this level, about four stores down from here on your right, just past the drugstore. |
   | Mari: | Thanks a lot! |
   | Clerk: | Yes? |
   | Woman: | Is there a hairdresser in this mall? |
   | Clerk: | Yes, there's one on the third floor. Take the escalator up two flights. |
   | Woman: | Thank you. |
   | Man: | I am looking for an umbrella. Where can I find them, please? |
   | Clerk: | The best place is Field's Department Store on the second floor. |

2. Ask these comprehension questions:

   - *What are they looking for?* (a women's clothing store, a hairdresser, a department store)
   - *Are there any women's clothing stores in the mall?* (yes, several)

3. Say: *Listen again. This time listen for the details of the conversation.*

4. Play or read the conversation again, pausing for choral repetition. Allow students to write down the information as they listen. Play or read the conversation again, if needed, for students to get all the information.

5. Ask the following questions:

   - *Where is the clothing store?* (on this level, four stores down on the right, just past the drugstore)
   - *Where is the hairdresser?* (on the third floor, up two flights)
   - *What does the man want?* (an umbrella)
   - *Where can he find one?* (in Field's Department Store, on the second floor)

   Elicit responses from various students.

## PRONUNCIATION FOCUS

**Class CD 1, Track 19**

1. Explain what the focus is. Read or play the examples in the book and have students repeat chorally.

   | | |
   |---|---|
   | **cl**othing | **dr**ugstore |
   | umbr**ella** | es**c**alator |

2. With books open, play or read the conversations again and have students pay attention to the consonant groups.

3. Paired Reading. Have students practice the conversations, switching roles.

## Give It a Try

Review. Name a place in your city or town. Ask a volunteer to describe the building and the location. Go rapidly around the classroom with different places.

## 1. Asking for directions in a store (1)

### Presentation

1. Have students look at the function box. Give them time to read the examples.

2. Model the exchange in the function box and have students repeat chorally.

### Notes

1. Explain that in the United States the first floor of a store is the floor that is at street level.

2. Point out that *Could you tell me where I can find an umbrella?* means the same as *Where can I find an umbrella?* but sounds a little more polite. Write both questions on the board and make sure students see the difference in the word order of *I can* and *can I* in the two questions.

### Practice

**Class CD 1, Track 20**

1. Have students read the directions and look at the list and the directory. Go over any vocabulary students don't know. Brainstorm the types of items or services available in each department, if necessary.

2. Play or read the example conversation.

   A: Could you tell me where I can find an umbrella?
   B: In the accessories department, on the second floor.

3. Pair Work. Have students take turns asking each other about where they can do each of the things on the list.

4. Have pairs demonstrate their exchanges for the class.

## 2. Asking for directions in a store (2)

### Presentation

1. Have students look at the function box. Give them time to read the examples.

2. Model the exchange in the function box and have students repeat chorally.

### Note

Review the placement of stress on content words. Remind students that words that carry the meaning or information in a sentence receive more stress. This is especially true in exchanges about directions. On the board, write these sentences without marking the stressed words:

   *I'm looking for gloves for my sister. Ladies gloves are here on the main floor. Walk down this aisle to the scarf counter and turn left.*

Ask volunteers to come to the board and mark which words should receive more stress. Model the sentences and have the class repeat chorally.

### Practice

**Class CD 1, Track 21**

1. Have students read the directions and look at the floor plan and the words in the box.

2. Play or read the example conversation.

   A: I'm looking for an umbrella. Where can I find them, please?
   B: Umbrellas are on this floor. Walk down here to your left. They're across from the perfume counter.

3. Pair Work. Have students take turns asking and answering questions about where they can buy the items listed in the word box.

4. Have various pairs demonstrate their conversation for the class.

### Extension

Have students use their dictionaries to add words to the **Use These Words** list.

## 3. Asking for directions in a mall

### Presentation

1. Have students look at the function box. Give them time to read the examples.

2. Model the exchanges in the function box and have students repeat chorally.

### Note

Remind students which words receive stress in an exchange about directions. On the board, write these sentences without the stress marked:

*Is there a <u>pharmacy</u> in this mall?*

*Where can I buy <u>toothpaste</u>?*

*The pharmacy is <u>four stores down</u> on the <u>left</u>.*

Have students identify which words will receive more stress. Model the sentences and have students repeat individually and chorally.

### Practice

**Class CD 1, Track 22**

1. Have students read the directions and look at the mall directory.

2. Read the names of the stores for the class and have students identify what type of store each one is.

3. Play or read the example conversation.

   A: I need to buy a new shirt. Where can I find a women's clothing store?
   B: There is a women's clothing store on this level.

4. Pair Work. Have students take turns asking and answering questions about places in the mall.

5. Have several pairs demonstrate their exchanges for the class.

### Extension

Divide the class into groups of three or four. Have each group write a conversation that has one or two people asking a person at a mall information booth questions about in which stores they can find various items and where those stores are located. Encourage students to be imaginative. For example: they have triplet grandchildren and are shopping for unusual birthday presents, or they are going on a trip to the Amazon jungle and need unusual items. Have groups perform their conversation for the class.

## Listen to This

**Class CD 1, Track 23**

### Part 1

1. Give students time to read the directions and look at the chart.

2. To check comprehension, ask:

   *What will you listen for first?* (what each person is looking for)

   *Where will you write it?* (in the first column)

3. Play or read the conversations twice. Have students fill in the item or service for each conversation.

   **1**
   M: Excuse me. Does your store sell running shoes? I was in the shoe department but I didn't see any running shoes...or sales clerks.
   C: I'm sorry about that. Our running shoes are in Sporting Goods.
   M: That makes sense. And where is that department?
   C: Sporting Goods is on two. The second floor.
   M: Thank you.

   **2**
   W: Excuse me. Where's your furniture department?
   C: It's on the sixth floor.
   W: Do they sell tables and chairs for outside?
   C: No. All our outdoor furniture is in the Garden Shop. But that's also on six. Just be sure to turn left when you get off the escalator.
   W: I will. Thanks very much.

   **3**
   C: Can I help you?
   M: Yes, please. I bought this stereo here last week, and it's not working properly. Where is your repair department?
   C: Take that to the electronics department, where you bought it. They'll take care of it for you.
   M: Back to the electronics department? OK. That's on the third floor, isn't it?
   C: Yes, that's right.

4. Check answers.

   **Answers:**
   1. running shoes
   2. tables and chairs for outside (outdoor furniture)
   3. repair department

**Part 2**

1. Give students time to read the directions.

2. To check comprehension, ask:

   *What will you listen for this time?* (the correct floor and name of the department)

   *Where will you write it?* (in the second and third columns)

3. Play or read the conversations again. Have students fill in the rest of the chart.

4. Check answers.

> **Answers:**
> 1. Sporting Goods; second floor
> 2. Garden Shop; sixth floor
> 3. electronics department; third floor

**Part 3**

1. Give students time to read the directions.

2. To check comprehension, ask:

   *What will you listen for this time?* (where each customer thought they would find the item or service)

3. Play or read the conversations again.

4. Pair Work. Have pairs discuss the questions.

5. Ask several pairs to tell their answers.

> **Answers:**
> 1. in the shoe department
> 2. in the furniture department
> 3. in the repair department

**Student Book pages 17 & 107**

## Person to Person

**Part 1**

1. Divide the class into pairs. Have students decide who will be Student A and who will be Student B. Remind Students B to look at page 107.

2. Have students read the directions and look at the map.

3. To check comprehension, ask Students A:

   *What is one thing you will ask Student B?* (Where can I buy books?)

4. Have pairs role-play the conversations. Circulate and help as needed.

**Part 2**

1. Have students read the directions.

2. Have Student B now ask Student A questions about where to find goods and services in the town.

3. Circulate and help students as needed.

## Now Try This

1. Have students read the directions.

2. Give them time to think of two or three places and how to describe them.

3. Pair Work. Have students take turns telling where a place is and how to recognize it.

4. Have pairs demonstrate for the class.

### Extension

Have students describe one place or building in their town, but not say what it is. Tell the other students to guess the place or building that is being described and what goods and services are provided there.

# Unit 3

## Could I please speak to Jo?

### Components

Student Book, pages 18–25, 108
Class CD 1, Tracks 24–35
Optional Activities 3.1–3.2,
pages 106–107

### Objectives

**Functions:** Asking to speak to someone, offering to take a message, taking a message, calling for information, asking for additional information, leaving a message

**Topics:** Talking on the telephone, getting information over the phone

**Structures:** Requests with *could*, use of *will* for offers

**Pronunciation Focus:** Stress placement on multisyllabic words

**Listen to This:** Listening for specific information: telephone conversations; filling in message forms and charts

---

Student Book page 18

## CONSIDER THIS

1. Have students read the text and the question.

2. Group Work. Divide students into groups of four or five. Have students in each group discuss their own text messaging and cell phone usage. Help students with vocabulary as needed.

3. Ask volunteers for their answers.

### Vocabulary

Introduce these phrases to the students:

*(my) place*: the place where one lives

*Are you free?*: Are you available?

*(See you Friday), then.*: in that case

*go ahead*: continue (talking)

*gets in*: arrives, comes back (to an enclosed place)

### Prelistening

1. Pair Work. Have students open their books and look at the photographs. Have partners describe what they see to each other. Circulate and help with vocabulary as needed.

2. Class Work. Read the title of the conversation and the prelistening questions. Ask volunteers to answer the questions.

## Conversation 1

**Class CD 1, Track 24**

1. With books closed, play the recording or read the conversations.

Jo: Hello.
Hong-an: Could I please speak to Jo?
Jo: Speaking.
Hong-an: Hi, Jo. This is Hong-an. Listen, I'm having a party at my place this Friday night. Are you free?
Jo: Sure! What time?
Hong-an: Anytime after 8:00.
Jo: Great! See you Friday, then.

Mrs. King: Hello?
Hong-an: Hi, Mrs. King. Is John there, please?
Mrs. King: I'm sorry, he's not here right now. Could I take a message?
Hong-an: Yes, please. I'm calling to tell him there's a party at my place on Friday, and...
Mrs. King: Just a moment. Let me get a pen.... All right, go ahead.
Hong-an: OK. This is Hong-an Li, and my number is 312-364-0107. Could you ask John to call me?
Mrs. King: Sure. I'll give him the message as soon as he gets in.

2. Ask these comprehension questions:

- *Why is Speaker 2 calling people?* (to invite them to his party)
- *How many phone calls does he make?* (two)
- *Who is at home?* (Jo)
- *Who isn't at home* (John)

3. Play or read the conversation again, pausing for choral repetition.

4. Ask the following questions:

- *Where is Speaker 1's party?* (at his home)
- *What day is the party?* (Friday)
- *What time is the party?* (anytime after 8:00)
- *Will Jo go?* (yes)
- *What is Speaker 1's phone number?* (312-364-0107)

Elicit responses from various students.

5. Paired Reading. Have students read the conversations, switching roles.

**Student Book page 19**

## Give It a Try

## 1. Asking to speak to someone

### *Presentation*

1. Have students look at the function boxes. Give them time to read the examples.

2. Model the exchanges and have students repeat chorally.

3. Practice a few exchanges with various students.

### Notes

1. Remind students that rising intonation is often used in requests. On the board, write the following sentences with marked intonation:

*Could I please speak to Jo?*

*Is Jo there, please?*

Model the phrases, emphasizing the rising intonation.

2. Point out that *Speaking.* is often used by the person being called on the telephone if the caller doesn't recognize the person's voice or the caller does not have an informal relationship with the person being called. Good friends can just say: *It's me.*

### *Practice 1*

**Class CD 1, Track 25**

1. Have students read the directions.

2. Play or read the example conversation twice.

    A: Hello.
    B: Hi. Could I please speak to Jo?
    A: Speaking.

3. Pair Work. Have students take turns role-playing calling each other on the telephone.

4. Ask several pairs to demonstrate for the class.

### *Practice 2*

**Class CD 1, Track 26**

1. Have students read the directions.

2. Play or read the example conversation twice.

    A: Hello.
    B: Hi. Is Jo there, please?
    A: Sure, just a moment, please. I'll get her.

3. Pair Work. Have students take turns role-playing telephoning another student in the class and answering and offering to get hold of the other person for the caller.

4. Ask several pairs to demonstrate for the class.

### *Extension*

Class discussion. Discuss with students phone etiquette in their culture. Talk about things such as: who is supposed to speak first, the caller or the person being called?, special telephone vocabulary or phrases, etc.

## 2. Offering to take a message

### *Presentation*

1. Have students look at the function box. Give them time to read the examples.

2. Model the exchanges and have students repeat chorally.

3. Practice a few exchanges with various students.

## Practice

Class CD 1, Track 27

1. Have students read the directions and look at the word box.

2. Play or read the example conversation twice.

   A: Hello.
   B: Hi, could I please speak to John?
   A: I'm sorry, he's not here right now. Could I take a message?
   B: No, thanks. I'll call back later.

3. Pair Work. Have students take turns role-playing calling someone and giving a reason why the person can't come to the phone and offering to take a message.

4. Ask several pairs to demonstrate for the class.

## Extension

Have students use their dictionaries to add other reasons to the **Use These Words** list.

**Student Book page 20**

## 3. Taking a message

### Presentation

1. Have students look at the function box. Give them time to read the examples.

2. Model the exchanges and have students repeat chorally.

3. Practice a few exchanges with various students.

### Notes

1. Explain that when taking a message, it is usual to repeat the details of the message back to the speaker.

2. Demonstrate "key spelling" when taking a message. Spell a student's last name (*Tanaka. T as in turtle, A as in apple*, etc.). Tell them that they can use any common word, as long as the first letter of the word clearly communicates the letter you are trying to confirm. Tell them that "key spelling" is often used on the phone by native speakers and is very useful with unfamiliar names and place names.

### Practice 1

Class CD 1, Track 28

1. Have students read the directions and look at the list.

2. Play or read the example conversation twice.

   A: Hello?
   B: Hi. Could I please speak to John?
   A: Sorry, he's not here right now. Can I take a message?
   B: Yes, please.
   A: Just a moment. Let me get a pen.... All right, go ahead.

B: This is Hong-an Li, and my number is 312-364-0107. Could you ask John to call me?
A: Sure. I'll give him the message as soon as he gets in.

3. Pair Work. Have students take turns role-playing calling and leaving a message, using the options on the list.

4. Ask several pairs to demonstrate for the class.

## Practice 2

1. Have students read the directions.

2. Give students time to think of their own message.

3. Pair Work. Have students take turns leaving a message and repeating the message back.

4. Ask several pairs to demonstrate for the class.

## Extension

Play Telephone. Put students into lines of four or five. Whisper the same phone message to each of the first students in line. Have them whisper the message to the person behind them and so on down the line. Have the last person write down the message. The first team to write down the message correctly wins. Vary the difficulty of the message depending on the level of your class.

## Listen to This

Class CD 1, Track 29

Part 1

1. Have students read the directions and look at the message notices.

2. Play or read the conversations. Tell students to listen for who the messages are for and who they are from.

   **1**
   Mrs. W: Hello?
   P:       Hello. Is Ted there, please?
   Mrs. W: I'm sorry. He isn't home right now. Could I take a message?
   P:       This is Pete Anderson. I'm calling about the school chess competition next weekend. Could you ask him to give me a call?
   Mrs. W: Sure. Does Ted have your number?
   P:       I'll give it to you just in case. It's 671-599-7671.
   Mrs. W: OK. 671-599-7671. Pete Anderson. About the chess competition.
   P:       That's it. Thank you.
   Mrs. W: You're welcome. Bye now.

**2**

Mrs. S: Hello?

E: Hi, Mrs. Samuels. This is Emma. Can I speak to Debbie, please?

Mrs. S: She's not in right now. Can I take a message?

E: Yes, please. Can you tell her the time of the test tomorrow has changed from 10:30 to 9:30? Mrs. Wilson phoned to tell me there was a mistake in the schedule.

Mrs. S: Oh, my goodness! That is important. Of course I'll tell her as soon as she gets in.

E: Thanks a lot.

Mrs. S: You're welcome. Good-bye, dear.

E: Good-bye.

3. Ask volunteers for their answers.

> **Answers:**
> 1. for Ted; from Pete Anderson
> 2. for Debbie; from Emma

### Part 2

1. Have students read the directions.

2. Play or read the conversations again and have students write the messages.

3. Play or read the conversations again for students to check their answers.

4. Ask volunteers for their answers.

> **Answers:**
> 1. Call Pete Anderson about the school chess competition at 671-599-7671.
> 2. The time of the exam tomorrow has changed from 10:30 to 9:30.

### Part 3

1. Have students read the directions.

2. Pair Work. Have partners discuss the possible relationships of the people in each conversation. Play the conversations again, if needed.

3. Ask volunteers for their answers.

> **Possible Answers:**
> 1. Ted may be the woman's son, brother, husband or just roommate. The caller may be a classmate of Ted.
> 2. Mrs. Samuels may be Debbie's mother. Emma may be a classmate of Debbie.

## Let's Talk

### Part 1

1. Have students read the directions.

2. Divide the class into groups.

3. Have students write their name on a piece of paper, fold it, and hand it to a student in another group.

### Part 2

1. Have students read the directions and look at the example messages. Go over any vocabulary students don't know. If necessary, discuss with students possible scenarios for why each message was left.

2. Give students time to write down a message to the person whose name is on the paper they received. Encourage students to think of funny or imaginative messages.

3. Circulate and help as needed.

### Part 3

1. Have students read the directions.

2. Pair Work. Have students sit back to back and take turns calling and leaving a message for the person on their paper while their partner writes the message down.

### Part 4

1. Have students read the directions.

2. Give students time to deliver the message they took to the correct person. Then have them find the person they "left" a message for and check if the message they received is correct.

3. Class Work. Have the students read the message they received for the class. Ask the class to vote for the most interesting message.

# I'm sorry. Her line is busy right now.

**Student Book page 22**

Review. Point to a student and give him or her a short message such as: *This is Mike. Please tell Mary to call me back about class tomorrow at 788-2460.* Have that student write down the message and give a short message to someone else in the class, who writes it down. Continue as time allows. Check students' messages for accuracy.

## Vocabulary

Introduce these words and phrases to the students:

*to reach:* to succeed in contacting (by telephone)

*admissions:* the department that admits students into a school or program

*to apply:* to make a request to enter (a school or program)

*application form:* the papers one must fill out to apply

*registration fee:* money paid to enroll in a course

*student housing:* living arrangements for students; dormitories

*get back to (somebody):* phone (somebody) back

## Prelistening

1. Have students open their books and look at the photograph. Ask:

   * *Is the man calling a friend?* (no)
   * *Where is he calling?* (an admissions office)

2. Pair Work. Read the title of the conversation and the prelistening question. Have students discuss the question and list the information they should always include when leaving a message.

3. Class Work. Have pairs share their answers with the class.

## Conversation 2

**Class CD 1, Track 30**

1. With books closed, play the recording or read the conversation.

   Voice: *You have reached the English Language Institute. For Admissions, press or say 1 now. If you know...*

   Woman: Good morning. Admissions Office. Can I help you?

   Hong-an: Yes, please. I am interested in taking a language class. Could you tell me how to apply?

   Woman: Yes, of course. You just need to fill out an application form and send it to us with the registration fee.

   Hong-an: Great. Could you send me a form, please? My name is Hong-an Li, H-o-n-g, (dash), a-n, L-i, and my address is 4211 South Main Street, Chicago, 60614.

   Woman: OK, we'll send that out to you right away.

   Hong-an: I'd also like some information about student housing.

   Woman: Sure, you can speak to our student housing coordinator. Hold on a moment, please. I'll see if she is available.... I'm sorry, her line is busy right now. Could I have your number?

   Hong-an: Yes, of course. My number is 312-364-0107.

   Woman: I'll see she gets back to you very soon.

2. Ask these comprehension questions:

   * *Where specifically is he calling?* (the English Language Institute)
   * *Why is he calling?* (to apply for a class)

3. Say: *Listen again. This time listen for the details of the conversation.*

4. Play or read the conversation again, pausing for choral repetition. Allow students to write down the information as they listen. Play or read the conversation again, if needed, for students to get all the information.

5. Ask the following questions:

   * *How does someone apply for a class?* (fill out an application form and send it to the Admissions Office with the registration fee)
   * *What is the man's name and address?* (Hong-an Li. 4211 South Main Street, Chicago, 60614.)
   * *What other information does the man want?* (information about student housing)
   * *Is the student housing coordinator available?* (no)
   * *What is the man's phone number?* (312-364-0107)

   Elicit responses from various students.

## PRONUNCIATION FOCUS

**Class CD 1, Track 31**

1. Explain what the focus is. Write the examples on the board and ask students to indicate the stressed syllables.

2. Play or read the examples in the book and have students repeat chorally.

| | | |
|---|---|---|
| 1st syllable: | institute | interested |
| 2nd syllable: | admissions | available |
| 3rd syllable: | application | registration |

3. With books open, play or read the conversation again. Tell students to pay attention to the stressed syllables.

4. Paired Reading. Have students practice the conversation, switching roles.

**Student Book page 23**

## Give It a Try

# 1. Calling for information

## Presentation

1. Have students look at the function box. Give them time to read the examples.

2. Model the exchanges and have students repeat chorally.

3. Practice some exchanges with various students.

## Practice

**Class CD 1, Track 32**

1. Have students read the directions and look at the list and the words and phrases in the box. Go over any vocabulary students don't know.

2. Play or read the example conversation twice.

    A: Good morning. Admissions Office. Can I help you?
    B: Yes, please. I am interested in taking a language class. Could you tell me how to apply?
    A: Yes, of course. You just need to fill out an application form and send it to us with the registration fee.
    B: Great. Could you send me a form, please? My name is Hong-an Li, H-o-n-g, (dash), a-n, L-i, and my address is 4211 South Main Street, Chicago, 60614.
    A: OK, we'll send that out to you right away.

3. Pair Work. Have students take turns asking each other for information about the things on the list.

4. Have pairs demonstrate their exchanges for the class.

# 2. Asking for additional information

## Presentation

1. Have students look at the function box. Give them time to read the examples.

2. Model the exchanges and have students repeat chorally.

## Practice

**Class CD 1, Track 33**

1. Have students read the directions and look at the list. Go over any vocabulary students don't know.

2. Play or read the example conversation twice.

    A: I'd also like some information about student housing, please.
    B: Sure, you can speak to our student housing coordinator. Hold on, please. I'll see if she is available.

3. Pair Work. Have students take turns asking each other for information about the things from the list in the previous Practice and asking for additional information using the new list.

4. Have various pairs demonstrate their conversation for the class.

## Extension

Have students use their dictionaries to add words to the **Use These Words** list.

## 3. Leaving a message

### Presentation

1. Have students look at the function box. Give them time to read the examples.

2. Model the exchanges and have students repeat chorally.

**Student Book page 24**

### Practice 1

**Class CD 1, Track 34**

1. Have students read the directions and look at the phone message memo and the lists.

2. Play or read the example conversation twice.

   A: I'm sorry, the housing coordinator's line is busy right now. Could I have your number?
   B: Yes, of course. My number is 312-364-0107.
   A: I'll see she gets back to you very soon.
   B: Thank you.

3. Pair Work. Have students take turns answering the phone and leaving a message.

4. Have several pairs demonstrate their exchanges for the class.

### Practice 2

1. Have students read the directions.

2. Give students time to think of three more situations where they would leave a formal message. If necessary, brainstorm various situations as a class.

3. Pair Work. Have students take turns answering the phone and leaving a message.

4. Have several pairs demonstrate their exchanges for the class.

## Listen to This

**Class CD 1, Track 35**

**Part 1**

1. Give students time to read the directions and look at the chart.

2. To check comprehension, ask:

   *What will you listen for first?* (what place and who or what department each person is calling)

   *Where will you write it?* (in the first and second columns)

3. Play or read the conversations twice. Have students fill in the places called and who the callers want to speak to.

**1**
M: Good afternoon. University of Miami.
F: Yes. Good afternoon. I'd like to speak to the Student Housing Office, please.
M: Hold the line. I'll connect you. I'm sorry. All the lines are busy right now. Could you call back later?
F: Sure. Thank you.

**2**
F: Good afternoon. Medical Clinic.
M: Is Dr. Adams available, please?
F: I'm sorry. He's on vacation this week. Can another doctor help you?
M: No, I don't think so. When will Dr. Adams be back in the office?
F: He'll be back on Monday morning.
M: OK. I'll call back then.

**3**
M: Computer City. How can I help you?
F: I'd like to speak to the technical support department, please.
M: Is there anyone in particular you want to speak to?
F: No. Just technical support. I only have one quick question.
M: OK. I'll put you through.

**4**
F: Global Travel. Good morning.
P: Good morning. Is Nancy Green there, please?
F: Yes, she's here, but she's with a customer right now. Can I take a message and have her call you back?
P: All right. My name is Peggy O'Hara, and my number is 361-444-1416.

4. Ask volunteers for their answers.

> **Answers:**
> 1. University of Miami; someone in the Student Housing Office
> 2. Medical Clinic; Dr. Adams
> 3. Computer City; someone in the technical support department
> 4. Global Travel; Nancy Green

## Part 2

1. Give students time to read the directions.

2. To check comprehension, ask:

   *What will you listen for this time?* (if the person they want to speak to is available)

   *Where will you write it?* (in the third column)

3. Play or read the conversations again. Have students fill in the rest of the chart.

4. Ask volunteers for their answers.

   **Answers:**
   1. no
   2. no
   3. yes
   4. no

## Part 3

1. Give students time to read the directions.

2. Play or read the conversations again and have students write any useful phrases.

3. Ask several volunteers to say the result of each conversation.

4. Ask students to say any useful phrases they heard. Make a master list on the board and have students copy it in their notebooks.

   **Answers:**
   1. The caller will call back later.
   2. The caller will call back on Monday (morning).
   3. The caller is put through.
   4. The caller leaves her name and number.

### *Extension*

Divide the class into pairs. Have students use the list of useful phrases to write their own extended phone conversations. Have pairs perform their role-play in front of the class.

**Student Book pages 25 & 108**

## Person to Person

### Part 1

1. Divide the class into pairs. Have students decide who will be Student A and who will be Student B. Remind Student B to look at page 108.

2. Have students read the instructions and look at the phone message memos.

3. To check comprehension, ask:

   *Student A, what is your role?* (receptionist at Soundz Eazy)

   *Student B, what is your role?* (Pete Saito, a musician with Sound Bite)

4. Have pairs role-play the conversation. Circulate and help as needed.

### Part 2

1. Have students read the directions.

2. To check comprehension, ask:

   *Student A, what will you do now?* (call Pete so he can arrange an audition)

   *Student B, what will you do now?* (pretend to be Pete's roommate, Chris, and take a message for Pete)

3. Have pairs role-play the conversation. Circulate and help as needed.

### Part 3

1. Have students read the directions.

2. To check comprehension, ask:

   *Student A, what will you do now?* (tell Pete how to get an audition)

   *Student B, what will you do now?* (call back Ed Black's office and ask for information about getting an audition and renting sound equipment and a studio)

3. Have pairs role-play the conversation. Circulate and help as needed.

## Now Try This

1. Have students read the directions.

2. Pair Work. Give pairs time to think of where they will call, what information they will ask for, and what information they will give. Circulate and help as needed.

3. Have pairs demonstrate their role-play for the class.

### *Extension*

If you have a high-level class, have students do spontaneous role-plays of telephone conversations. Point to one student, give them one minute to think of where they will call and what they will ask for, and have them role-play a telephone conversation with another student. Then give that student one minute to think of where to call and what to ask for, and so on.

# Review:
## Units 1–3

**Components**

Student Book, pages 26–27
Class CD 1, tracks 36–38

**Student Book page 26**

## Listen To This Unit 1

Class CD 1, Track 36

1. Have students read the directions and look at the questions.

2. Play or read the conversation.

> T: I hope this class won't be too difficult. I'm not good at math.
> S: Neither am I. You know, I think we've met somewhere before, haven't we?
> T: I'm not sure. Have we?
> S: Weren't you in that history class last semester with Mr. Smith?
> T: Yeah, I was.
> S: Yes, you sat in the front row. I was two rows behind. You probably didn't see me. Anyway, my name's Sophie. Nice to meet you.
> T: Nice to meet you, too. I'm Tran.
> S: Do you want to go for a coffee after class today?
> T: That would be nice.

3. Have students answer the questions.

4. Ask volunteers for their answers.

> **Answers:**
> 1. In a classroom.
> 2. In history class last semester.
> 3. Sophie and Tran.
> 4. Sophie recognized Tran, but Tran didn't recognize Sophie.

## Give It a Try

1. Have students read the directions.

2. Pair Work. Give students time to choose two famous people. Have them write a conversation between the two people talking about how they met and what they have done recently. Make sure they don't use the famous people's names.

3. Class Work. Have students role-play the conversation for the class. Ask the other students to guess who the students are pretending to be.

4. Have the class vote on the best, most imaginative conversation

## Listen To This Unit 2

Class CD 1, Track 37

1. Have students read the directions and look at the questions and the floor plan.

2. Play or read the conversations.

> **1**
> Turn right at the next corner. Keep walking past the food court, turn right again, it's next to the coffee shop.
>
> **2**
> Turn right at the bookstore, keep going until you see the toy store, it's about three stores down, on your right.
>
> **3**
> It's across from the juice bar, between the jeans and the sports clothing store. You can't miss it.

3. Have students answer the questions

4. Ask volunteers for the answers.

> **Answers:**
> 1. Clicker Camera
> 2. Short Cuts Hair Salon
> 3. Bed and Bath Shop

**Student Book page 27**

## Give It a Try

1. Have students read the directions and look at the chart.

2. Group Work. Give students time to choose four useful stores in their town or city. Then have them fill in the chart with the information about each store.

3. Have each group report their discussion to the class.

### Extension

Have the class discuss what stores or services are missing from their town or city and what stores there are too many of.

## Listen To This Unit 3

Class CD 1, Track 38

1. Have students read the directions and look at the message forms.

2. Play or read the messages.

**1**

V: Hi. You have reached the Johnson's. We can't come to the phone right now, but if you leave your name, number, and a brief message, we'll get back to you as soon as we can.

D: This is a message for Mrs. Johnson. This is Debbie. I can't baby-sit on Friday night, but a friend of mine can if you want. She has lots of experience baby-sitting. Her name is Mary Ann, and her phone number is, uh, 209-892-2971. Bye.

**2**

V: Hi. This is Dave Summers. I can't talk right now, but leave your name, number, and a brief message and I'll call you back.

R: Hi, Dave, this is Ron. Something's come up and I can't make it to the show tomorrow night. You're going to be mad at me, I know, but listen, Barry says he can play the bass for some of our tunes. He's heard us playing them enough times! Give him a try. His number is 677-439-2121.

**3**

V: Hi. This is Michiko Saito. I can't come to the phone right now, but if you leave your name, number, and a message, I'll call you back as soon as I can.

T: Hi, Michi…this is Tammy…want to come to a party on Friday night? Call me if you can, 607-690-2541.

3. Have students fill in the forms.

4. Ask volunteers for their answers.

> **Answers:**
> 1. For Mrs. Johnson; From Debbie; She can't baby sit on Friday night, but Mary Ann can. Her number is 209-892-2971
> 2. For Dave; From Ron; He can't make it to the show tomorrow night. Barry can play the bass to some of the tunes. His number is 677-439-2121
> 3. For Michiko; From Tammy; Come to a party Friday night. Call her at 607-690-2541 if you can.

## Give It a Try

1. Have students read the directions and look at the flyers.

2. Give students time to think of three questions to ask when they call each place.

3. Pair Work. Have students take turns calling each place and asking for information.

4. Have pairs demonstrate their conversations for the class.

# What can we do?

## Components

Student Book, pages 28–35, 109
Class CD 1, Tracks 39–47
Optional Activities 4.1–4.2,
page 107

## Objectives

**Functions:** Identifying a problem, making suggestions, asking for and giving advice, describing consequences

**Topics:** Public and private issues, solutions, and consequences

**Structures:** Modal verbs *can, would, should,* conditionals, *Why don't…?*

**Pronunciation Focus:** Intonation in Wh-questions and Yes/No questions

**Listen to This:** Listening for specific information: problems and solutions, problems and advice; filling in charts

---

**Student Book page 28**

## CONSIDER THIS

1. Have students read the text and the question.

2. Group Work. Divide students into groups of four or five. Have students in each group discuss which everyday inventions they hate but can't live without. Help students with vocabulary as needed.

3. Ask volunteers for their answers.

### Vocabulary

Introduce these phrases to the students:

*while (class) is going on*: during (class)

*fine*: money paid as punishment after you break a rule or a law

*Like (how much?)*: often used as a filler word in spoken conversation

*end-of-semester party*: a party to celebrate the end of a school term

### Prelistening

1. Pair Work. Have students open their books and look at the photograph. Have partners describe what they see to each other. Circulate and help with vocabulary as needed.

2. Class Work. Read the title of the conversation and the prelistening questions and task. Ask volunteers to answer the questions.

## Conversation 1

**Class CD 1, Track 39**

1. With books closed, play the recording or read the conversations.

Jane: Is that your cell phone? It's really loud!

Pat: Yeah–sorry, just a minute, I'll turn it off.

Jane: You know, it's really a problem when people bring their cell phones to class. Some students even answer their phones and have conversations while class is going on!

Jim: I know what you mean. It's not polite and it disturbs everyone. What can we do?

Jane: We can have a sign up on the wall, like they do in the movie theater, that says, "Remember to turn off your cell phones."

Pat: That's a good idea, but maybe we could put the sign on the door so you see it before you come into class.

Jim: Let's have a fine for anyone whose phone rings in class.

Pat: Oh, yeah? Like how much? And who would collect the money? That's too complicated.

Jim: We can have a box, and when your phone rings, you put in a quarter. How does that sound?

Pat: Yeah, we can use it to buy drinks for the end-of-semester party!

Jane: Leave it to you to think of that.

2. Ask these comprehension questions:

- *What is really loud?* (Speaker 2's cell phone)
- *Where are Speakers 1, 2, and 3?* (in a classroom)

3. Play or read the conversation again, pausing for choral repetition.

4. Ask the following questions:

- *What do the speakers think is a problem?* (when people bring cell phones to class)
- *What does Speaker 1 suggest?* (putting a sign up)
- *What does Speaker 2 suggest?* (having a fine)
- *What does Speaker 3 suggest?* (having a box where offenders put in a quarter)
- *What does Speaker 2 want to do with the money?* (buy drinks for an end-of-semester party)

Elicit responses from various students.

5. Paired Reading. Have students read the conversation, switching roles.

**Student Book page 29**

## Give It a Try

# 1. Identifying a problem

## *Presentation*

1. Have students look at the function box. Give them time to read the examples.

2. Model the exchanges and have students repeat chorally.

3. Have some pairs practice the exchanges with different combinations.

## Notes

1. Remind students that stress is given to the content words in a sentence. Content words are the nouns, verbs, adjectives, and adverbs. These words are said louder and held longer. Other parts of a sentence, auxiliary verbs, articles, pronouns, and prepositions, are usually not stressed.

2. Explain to students that the use of cell phones in some public places is restricted. It is also considered bad manners to talk on a cell phone in any public place where talking would disturb the other people there. At concerts, restaurants, libraries, and movie theaters, people generally turn off their phones so they won't ring.

3. *I know what you mean* indicates agreement and understanding of another's point of view. In contrast, saying *I don't know what you mean* tells the other person that they need to explain their viewpoint more clearly. *Absolutely* indicates strong agreement.

## *Practice 1*

**Class CD 1, Track 40**

1. Have students read the directions and look at the pictures and the word box. Ask questions about the pictures and go over vocabulary, if necessary.

2. Play or read the example conversation twice.

   A: It's really a problem when people bring their cell phones to class.

   B: I know what you mean. It's not polite and it disturbs everyone.

3. Pair Work. Have students take turns talking about why using a cell phone in each of the situations depicted might be a problem.

4. Ask several pairs to demonstrate for the class.

## *Practice 2*

1. Have students read the directions.

2. Give students time to think of other situations where using a cell phone might be a problem.

3. Pair Work. Have students take turns talking about using a cell phone in the new situations.

4. Ask several pairs to demonstrate for the class.

## *Practice 3*

1. Have students read the directions and look at the list of ideas. Brainstorm and discuss more ideas, if necessary.

2. Pair Work. Have students discuss problems in their school

3. Ask several pairs to demonstrate for the class.

## *Extension*

1. Class discussion. Make a list on the board of the problems that students discussed in Practice 3. Continue these discussions as a class and have students think of ways the situations can be improved.

2. Have students use their dictionaries to add words to the **Use These Words** list.

## 2. Making suggestions

### Presentation

1. Have students look at the function box. Give them time to read the examples.

2. Model the exchanges and have students repeat chorally.

3. Practice a few exchanges with various students.

**Student Book page 30**

### Practice 1

**Class CD 1, Track 41**

1. Have students read the directions.

2. Play or read the example conversation twice.

> A: What can we do about students using cell phones in class?
> B: We can have a sign on the wall that says, "Remember to turn off your cell phones."
> A: That's a good idea.
> C: Let's have a fine for anyone whose cell phone rings in class.
> B: That's too complicated.

3. Group Work. Divide the class into groups of three. Have students look at the pictures from Practice 1 in Part 1. Tell one student to ask about a solution, have the other two make a suggestion, and have the first student say if it's a good solution or not. Brainstorm possible solutions before the students' discussions, if necessary.

4. Ask several groups to demonstrate for the class.

### Practice 2

1. Have students read the directions and look at the pictures and the captions.

2. Group Work. Have students discuss problems in their neighborhood or town and possible solutions.

3. Ask several groups to demonstrate for the class.

## Listen to This

**Class CD 1, Track 42**

Part 1

1. Have students read the directions and look at the chart.

2. Play or read the talk. Tell students to listen for the four main problems with the environment mentioned and write them in the chart.

> Good evening, ladies and gentlemen, and welcome. I'm sure we have all heard the expression, "Think Green." Tonight we are going to talk about ways that we can "Act Green" in our everyday lives.

The best place to start, of course, is in the home. Every day, people all over the world are hurting the environment without even knowing it. For example, busy families buy paper napkins and towels at the supermarket. This helps them save time on housework, but after these things have been used, what happens to them? They go in the trash. In many places, especially in North America, big cities are running out of places to throw their trash. What can we do about this? How can we cut down on garbage?

Well, we can start using cloth napkins and cloth towels instead of paper towels. When we go grocery shopping, we can choose products that are not overpackaged. For example, last week I bought a package of cookies. The cookies were in a bag, there was a plastic tray inside the bag, and then each cookie was in its own little package on the tray in the bag! That's overpackaging! We should also take our own bags to the grocery store to carry things home in.

Cleaning products are another danger. Dangerous cleaning products enter our water supply every day. Of course, everyone wants a clean house—so what's the answer? For one thing, we could make our own cleaning products from natural ingredients like baking soda, lemon, and vinegar.

Now, how about in the community? At work and school, we use one very valuable item every day. Paper. Of course, we need paper to do our work, but how much do we waste? Get your school or office to recycle paper. Learn to make notepads from the unused sides of old pieces of paper. Finally, plant a tree. Better yet, plant two trees!

3. Play or read the talk again for students to check their answers.

4. Ask volunteers for the answers.

> **Answer:**
> 1. Big cities are running out of places to throw trash.
> 2. Overpackaging of products.
> 3. Dangerous cleaning products in our water.
> 4. Wasting paper.

## Part 2

1. Have students read the directions.

2. Play or read the talk again and tell students to listen for the solutions and write them in the chart.

3. Play or read the talk again for students to check their answers.

4. Ask volunteers for the answers.

> **Answers:**
> 1. Use cloth napkins and towels.
> 2. Choose products that are not overpackaged. Take your own bags to the grocery store.
> 3. Use cleaning products made from natural ingredients.
> 4. Reuse and recycle paper; plant trees.

## Part 3

1. Have students read the directions.

2. Pair Work. Have partners discuss what "think green" means.

3. Ask volunteers for their answers.

> **Possible Answers:**
> Think about environmental issues.
> Think how you can avoid creating environmental problems.

## Extension

Class Discussion. Discuss with students which environmental issues are the most important to them. Discuss how these problems can be solved.

## Let's Talk

### Part 1

1. Have students read the directions for the activity.

2. Divide the class into groups.

3. Group Work. Give students time to think of a problem in the school that affects everyone and three reasons why it is a problem. Have them write their reasons in the chart. Brainstorm problems in the school, if necessary. Make sure that students pick a problem that has possible solutions.

4. Circulate and help as needed.

### Part 2

1. Have students read the directions.

2. Group Work. Give students time to think of three possible solutions to their problem and reasons why each solution might or might not work. Have them write their solutions and reasons in the chart. Then they should vote on the best solution.

3. Circulate and help as needed.

### Part 3

1. Have students read the directions.

2. Class Work. Have one person from each group report on their group's discussion. Have the other students discuss if they agree or disagree with their solutions. Make sure they support their answers.

## Extension

Have students write a letter to the head of the school outlining one or two of the problems discussed, who it affects, and a solution.

# What would you do?

Student Book page 32

## Vocabulary

Introduce these words and phrases to the students:

*What's the problem?*: What's the matter?

*the cheapest (guy)*: a person who does not like to spend money; not generous

*to go out with*: to socialize with someone in a romantic way

*snack bar*: place (in a movie theater) that sells fast food and drinks

## Prelistening

1. Have students open their books and look at the photograph. Ask:

   • *How does the woman seem?* (confused, upset)

2. Pair Work. Read the title of the conversation and the prelistening questions. Have students discuss the questions with their partners.

3. Class Work. Have pairs share their answers with the class.

## Conversation 2

**Class CD 1, Track 43**

1. With books closed, play the recording or read the conversation.

   Jim: OK, Tamara, what's the problem?

   Tamara: Oh...I don't know.

   Jim: Come on, I'm your friend—do you want to talk about it?

   Tamara: OK. It's Ken. He's really fun to be with, but he's the cheapest guy I've ever gone out with.

   Jim: Why? What did he do?

   Tamara: Last night we went to a movie. I bought the tickets while he parked the car.

   Jim: So?

   Tamara: Well, he never gave me any money for his ticket. Then he went to the snack bar and came back with popcorn and soda...for himself! He never even asked me if I wanted anything!

   Jim: Wow! That sounds pretty bad.

   Tamara: I know. I really like him, but he makes me so mad. What should I do?

   Jim: You should start looking for a new boyfriend!

2. Ask these comprehension questions:

   • *What is the relationship of the speakers?* (friends)
   • *What are they talking about?* (Speaker 2 has a problem with her boyfriend.)

3. Say: *Listen again. This time listen for what happened last night.*

4. Play or read the conversation again, pausing for choral repetition. Allow students to write down the information as they listen. Play or read the conversation again, if needed, for students to get all the information.

5. Ask the following questions:

   • *Where did Speaker 2 and her boyfriend go last night?* (to a movie)

   • *Did he pay for the movie?* (no, she did)

   • *What did he buy at the snack bar?* (soda and popcorn)

   • *Why was Speaker 2 angry?* (He did not buy any for her.)

   • *What advice does Speaker 1 give her?* (She should look for a new boyfriend.)

   Elicit responses from various students.

## PRONUNCIATION FOCUS

**Class CD 1, Track 44**

1. Explain what the focus is. Write the examples on the board. Play or read the examples in the book and have students repeat chorally. Have students indicate the intonation of each question on the board with falling or rising arrows.

   **What's the problem?**
   **Do you want to talk about it?**

2. With books open, play or read the conversation again. Tell students to pay attention to the intonation of the questions.

3. Paired Reading. Have students practice the conversation, switching roles.

## Give It a Try

# 1. Asking for and giving advice

## Presentation

1. Have students look at the function box. Give them time to read the examples.

2. Model the exchanges and have students repeat chorally.

3. Practice a few exchanges with various students.

### Note

*What should I do?* is used when asking someone for advice. *What would you do?* is used when you want to know what another person would do if they were in your situation.

## Practice 1

**Class CD 1, Track 45**

1. Have students read the directions and look at the lists. Go over any vocabulary students don't know.

2. Play or read the example conversation.

   A: What's the problem?
   B: Ken is the cheapest guy I've ever gone out with. What should I do?
   A: You should start looking for a new boyfriend!

3. Discuss which solutions go with which problems. Also, ask students if they can think of any other solutions for the problems.

4. Pair Work. Have students decide who will be Student A and who will be Student B. Have Student B tell Student A about a problem and Student A give advice.

5. Have pairs demonstrate their exchanges for the class.

## Practice 2

1. Have students read the directions and look at the lists. Go over any vocabulary students don't know.

2. Discuss which solutions go with which problems. Also, ask students if they can think of any other solutions for the problems.

3. Pair Work. Have students switch roles and practice talking about a problem and giving advice.

4. Have pairs demonstrate their exchanges for the class.

## Extension

1. Have students sit in a circle. Write different problems on separate slips of paper and put them in a box or bag. Have one student choose a paper and ask the student next to him or her for advice. Then have the student who gave advice choose a paper. Continue as quickly as you can around the circle.

2. Have students write a problem on a slip of paper, but not tell anyone what their problem is. Encourage students to come up with imaginative or humorous problems. Collect the papers. Have a student choose one of the papers, read it to the class, and give advice.

# 2. Describing consequences

## Presentation

1. Have students look at the function box. Give them time to read the examples.

2. Model the exchanges and have students repeat chorally.

## Practice 1

**Class CD 1, Track 46**

1. Have students read the directions.

2. Review the problems and possible solutions from the previous Practices.

3. Play or read the example conversation.

   A: What's the problem?
   B: Ken is the cheapest guy I've ever gone out with. What should I do?
   A: Why don't you talk to him about it?
   B: If I criticize him, he'll get mad at me!
   A: In that case, I think you should start looking for a new boyfriend!

4. Pair Work. Have students take turns giving advice, describing possible consequences of the advice, and giving new advice. Practice a few exchanges as a class, if necessary.

5. Have various pairs demonstrate their conversation for the class.

## Practice 2

1. Have students read the directions and look at the word box. Give students time to think of an everyday problem.

2. Group Work. Divide the class into groups. Have students in the group take turns telling their problem to the others and getting advice from them. Have them respond to each suggestion.

3. Have each group demonstrate one or two of their conversations to the class.

## Extension

Have students use their dictionaries to add responses to the **Use These Words** list.

## Listen to This

Class CD 1, Track 47

### Part 1

1. Give students time to read the directions and look at the chart.

2. Tell students to listen for each of the problems and write them in the chart.

3. Play or read the conversations twice.

**1**

F: Hi, Luisa.

L: Hi.

F: What's the matter?

L: I have a problem with my mom.

F: Do you want to talk about it?

L: Well…my mother said I can't go to David's birthday party on Thursday night.

F: How come?

L: Because it's a school night and I have some big tests next week. She wants me to stay home and study. I really want to go. I don't know what to do.

F: Why don't you promise to come home early?

**2**

J: …and then we'll go for coffee. Is that OK with you, Elaine? Elaine? Are you listening?

E: What? Oh, sorry. What did you say?

J: What's the problem, Elaine? Are you worried about something?

E: It's my boyfriend. He wants to go and live in Australia.

J: Does he have a job over there or something?

E: Yes, he does and he wants me to go, too.

J: Do you want to go?

E: That's the problem. I'm not sure if I want to or not.

J: Well, maybe you should talk it over with your family. That might help you to decide.

**3**

M: That Brendan is driving me crazy!

T: Why? What's the matter?

M: He's always borrowing little things, and he never returns them.

T: Like what?

M: Oh, you know, pencils, paper, money for a coffee, bus tickets—I'm starting to feel like his mother! What would you do?

T: Well, I'd tell him you're sorry, but you just can't keep on giving stuff to him any more.

M: I guess you're right.

4. Check answers.

> **Answers:**
> 1. Luisa's mother won't let her go to a birthday party.
> 2. Emma's boyfriend wants to live in Australia.
> 3. Her friend Brendan keeps borrowing things and never returning them.

### Part 2

1. Give students time to read the directions.

2. Tell students to listen for the advice to each problem this time and write them in the chart.

3. Play or read the conversations again.

4. Ask volunteers for the answers.

> **Answers:**
> 1. Promise to come home early.
> 2. Talk it over with your family.
> 3. Say you are sorry and don't lend him things anymore.

### Part 3

1. Give students time to read the directions.

2. Play or read the conversations again and have students write what questions were asked to find out the problem.

3. Ask several volunteers for the answers.

> **Answers:**
> 1. What's the matter? Do you want to talk about it?
> 2. What's the problem? Are you worried about something?
> 3. What's the matter?

## Person to Person

**Part 1**

1. Divide the class into pairs. Have students decide who will be Student A and who will be Student B. Remind Students B to look at page 109.

2. Have students read the instructions and look at the pictures.

3. To check comprehension, ask:

   *Student A, what is your role?* (a person with a problem)

   *Student B, what is your role?* (a counselor)

4. Have pairs role-play the conversation. Make sure Student A writes down the advice from Student B. Circulate and help as needed.

**Part 2**

1. Have students read the directions.

2. To check comprehension, ask:

   *Student A, what will you do now?* (be the counselor)

   *Student B, what will you do now?* (talk to my partner about my problem)

3. Have pairs role-play the conversation. Make sure Student B writes down the advice from Student A. Circulate and help as needed.

**Part 3**

1. Have students read the directions.

2. Pair Work. Tell students to discuss the advice they were given by their partner and give specific reasons why it would or would not work. Circulate and help as needed.

3. Have pairs report their conversations to the class.

## Now Try This

1. Have students read the directions. Give students time to think of a problem they had and how it was resolved.

2. Pair Work. Have pairs take turns telling each other the problem, but not the result, and giving advice.

3. Have students tell each other if the advice from the other student was what they ended up doing.

4. Have pairs report their discussion to the class.

## Components

Student Book, pages 36–43
Class CD 1, Tracks 48–58
Optional Activities 5.1–5.2,
pages 107–108

## Objectives

**Functions:** Asking about other people, reacting to good and bad news, asking for more details, saying what someone should have done, interrupting and getting back to the story

**Topics:** Life events and problems

**Structures:** Present perfect, simple past, past continuous, future with *be going to*, *should* + perfect infinitive (*should have done*), adverbs of time and manner, strong adjectives

**Pronunciation Focus:** Stressed and unstressed words in sentences

**Listen to This:** Listening for gist, making inferences: topics of conversations; filling in a chart; listening for specific information: order of events, specific questions; ordering pictures

---

**Student Book page 36**

## CONSIDER THIS

1. Have students read the text and the question.

2. Group Work. Divide students into groups of four or five. Have students in each group discuss how they keep in touch with old friends and classmates. Help students with vocabulary as needed.

3. Ask volunteers for their answers.

### Vocabulary

Introduce these phrases to the students:

*How are things (with her)?*: How is (she)?

*so-so*: not great, but not terrible

*drop out of*: to quit school or a program

*You're kidding!*: expression of surprise or shock after hearing good or bad news

### Prelistening

1. Pair Work. Have students open their books and look at the photograph. Have partners describe what they see to each other. Circulate and help with vocabulary as needed.

2. Class Work. Read the title of the conversation and the prelistening questions. Ask volunteers to answer the questions.

## Conversation 1

**Class CD 1, Track 48**

1. With books closed, play the recording or read the conversation.

Young-hee: Have you heard about Eun-mi?
Jung-soo:  No, I haven't talked to her in a while. How are things with her?
Young-hee: Well, so-so. She broke her arm.
Jung-soo:  That's terrible. How did it happen?
Young-hee: Well, she went skiing during winter vacation. She had a bad fall and broke her arm.
Jung-soo:  That doesn't sound so good, but I'm glad it wasn't worse. How's she doing with her schoolwork?
Young-hee: Haven't you heard yet? She's decided to drop out of college and become a musician.
Jung-soo:  You're kidding! What made her decide to do that?
Young-hee: Well, you know that CD she made in her home recording studio? She sent it to a record company and they're giving her a contract!
Jung-soo:  That's great news! Good for her. Maybe she'll be on TV soon!

2. Ask these comprehension questions:

• *Who are the speakers talking about?* (Eun-mi)
• *What do you think is their relationship to her?* (friends)

3. Play or read the conversation again, pausing for choral repetition.

4. Ask the following questions:
   - *What bad thing happened to Eun-mi?* (She broke her arm.)
   - *How did it happen?* (She fell while she was skiing.)
   - *Is Eun-mi in school?* (Not any more; she dropped out.)
   - *What did she decide to do?* (become a musician)
   - *Why did she decide to become a musician?* (A recording company heard her CD and is going to give her a contract.)

   Elicit responses from various students.

5. Paired Reading. Have students read the conversation, switching roles.

**Student Book page 37**

## Give It a Try

## 1. Asking about other people

### Presentation

1. Have students look at the function boxes. Give them time to read the examples.

2. Model the exchanges and have students repeat chorally.

3. Practice a few exchanges with various students.

### Notes

1. Explain that the adjectives *great*, *pretty good*, etc. cover a wide range from very positive to fairly negative:

   The expression *not too good* (sometimes *not too great*) indicates that the speaker has some bad news to say, but doesn't want to alarm the listener.

   *So-so* means that things are not very bad, but they're not great, either.

   *Not bad* means that things are better than expected.

2. In rapid speech, *How's she* is pronounced /how'zshe/. On the board write the following and mark the blending:

   *How's she doing?*

   Model the example and have students repeat.

3. Sometimes, one of the questions in the first function box is enough to elicit information about someone. However, if the answer to those questions is negative, the other person will almost always ask a follow-up question, such as *Why? What happened?*, or *What's happening with him/her?*

### Practice

**Class CD 1, Track 49**

1. Have students read the directions and look at the pictures and the captions. Ask questions about the pictures and go over vocabulary, if necessary.

2. Play or read the example conversation twice.

   A: Have you heard about Eun-mi?
   B: No, I haven't. How's she doing these days?
   A: So-so.

3. Pair Work. Have students take turns asking and answering questions about he people in each picture.

4. Ask several pairs to demonstrate for the class.

## 2. Reacting to good and bad news

### Presentation

1. Have students look at the function boxes. Give them time to read the examples.

2. Model the exchanges and have students repeat chorally.

3. Practice a few exchanges with various students.

### Practice

**Class CD 1, Track 50**

1. Have students read the directions. Brainstorm what good or bad news relates to the pictures in the previous Practice, if necessary.

2. Play or read the example conversation twice.

   A: Have you heard about Eun-mi?
   B: How's she doing these days?
   A: So-so. She broke her arm.
   B: That's terrible.

3. Pair Work. Have students take turns asking and answering questions about the people in the previous Practice.

4. Ask several pairs to demonstrate for the class.

### Extension

Bring in magazine pictures of people in various situations. Show the pictures to the students and have pairs choose one picture and write their own conversations asking and answering questions about the people in the pictures. Have pairs demonstrate their conversation for the class. For a higher level class, show a pair a picture and have them spontaneously have a conversation about the picture. Continue with other pairs and different pictures.

# 3. Asking for more details

Review. Give a prompt such as *Susan/married*. Point to two students and ask them to have a short conversation with one student asking about Susan and the other giving news about her. Continue with other prompts and other pairs.

## Presentation

1. Have students look at the function boxes. Give them time to read the examples.

2. Model the exchanges and have students repeat chorally.

3. Practice a few exchanges with various students.

## Practice 1

**Class CD 1, Track 51**

1. Have students read the directions and look at the pictures and the word box. Ask questions about the pictures and go over vocabulary, if necessary.

2. Play or read the example conversation twice.

   A: How's Eun-mi doing these days?
   B: So-so. She broke her arm.
   A: That's terrible. How did it happen?
   B: Well, she went skiing during the winter vacation....

3. Pair Work. Have students take turns asking questions and giving more information about the people in the pictures.

4. Ask several pairs to demonstrate for the class.

## Practice 2

1. Have students read the directions.

2. Brainstorm famous people and possible questions to ask about them. Tell students that the information does not have to be true.

3. Pair Work. Have students take turns asking and answering questions about a famous person.

4. Ask several pairs to demonstrate for the class.

## Extension

Have students use their dictionaries to add words and expressions to the **Use These Words** list.

## Listen to This

**Class CD 1, Track 52**

### Part 1

1. Have students read the directions and look at the chart.

2. Play or read the conversations. Tell students to listen for the main topics and write them in the chart.

**1**
S: Have you heard what happened to Ellen's parents?
P: No, what happened?
S: The roof of their house was blown off by a tornado.
P: That's awful! Are they OK? Where are they going to live?
S: They are fine. They're staying with Ellen's brother right now. What's really bad is that the house wasn't covered by insurance.
P: Oh, that's really bad news.

**2**
J: Have you heard about Steve?
S: No, what happened to him?
J: Well, he applied for a job as a script assistant at a big movie company. He had to take some sort of test.
S: A test? What kind of test?
J: Oh, I don't know, some kind of grammar or spelling test, I suppose. Anyway, he failed the test, but they gave him a job as a movie extra instead. Isn't that great?
S: Good for him! So he'll be in the movies now?
J: Yeah, he's really ecstatic.

**3**
N: What's going on with Dan these days? I haven't seen him for a while.
G: Well, he hasn't been too good recently. You know he lost his job, don't you?
N: Oh, no! Why? What happened?
G: His company went bankrupt. They didn't even pay him his last month's salary.
N: That's too bad. What's he going to do now?
G: He couldn't decide what to do at first, but I think he's going to move to California and look for a job out there.
N: I hope it works out.

3. Play or read the conversations again for students to check their answers.

4. Ask volunteers for the answers.

> **Answers:**
> 1. The roof of Ellen's parents' house was blown off by a tornado.
> 2. Steve got a job as a movie extra.
> 3. Dan lost his job.

## Part 2

1. Have students read the directions.

2. Play or read the conversations again and tell students to listen for information which indicates if the news is good or bad in each conversation.

3. Play or read the conversations again for the students to check their answers.

4. Ask volunteers for the answers.

> **Answers:**
> 1. bad news
> 2. good news
> 3. bad news

## Part 3

1. Have students read the directions.

2. Tell students to listen to the conversations again and write down the words or phrases that indicate good or bad news.

3. Ask volunteers for their answers.

> **Answers:**
> 1. That's awful! Oh, that's really bad news.
> 2. Isn't that great? Good for him! He's really ecstatic.
> 3. Oh, no! That's too bad.

## *Extension*

Class Discussion. Discuss with students how people talk about good or bad news in their culture. Is it polite to talk about your own good news? Is it impolite to talk about other people?

## Let's Talk

### Part 1

1. Have students read the directions.

2. Divide the class into pairs.

3. Give students time to think of a piece of good news and a piece of bad news about themselves. Tell them that the news does not have to be true.

4. Pair Work. Have students take turns asking and answering questions about their news.

5. Make sure students ask for details and pay attention to these. Circulate and help as needed.

### Note

Explain to students that they need to be sensitive when asking questions about someone's bad news. If the other person seems at all uncomfortable, they should stop asking questions and change the subject. A good idea is to ask the other person, "Do you want to talk about it?" If they answer "no", then they should drop the subject immediately. If time allows, role-play a situation like this with students.

### Part 2

1. Have students read the directions.

2. Pair Work. Have students pair with a new student. Have them take turns asking and answering questions about the news from their first partner.

3. Circulate and help as needed.

### Part 3

1. Have students read the directions.

2. Class Work. Ask several students about the news that they heard from their first partners. Have the students ask their first partners if the information they are giving to the class is correct.

# Wait a minute. Was she hurt?

Student Book page 40

## Vocabulary

Introduce these words and phrases to the students:

*to catch* (someone doing something): to discover by accident

*poor* (woman): pitiful

*Let me get this straight.*: Let me make sure that I understand correctly.

*soap opera*: a type of continuing drama on TV in which characters have a variety of personal problems and romances

## Prelistening

1. Have students open their books and look at the photograph. Ask:

   • *What do you think is the relationship of the two women?* (friends)
   • *What do you think they are talking about?* (One of them is telling a shocking story.)

2. Pair Work. Read the title of the conversation and the prelistening questions. Have students discuss the questions with their partners.

3. Class Work. Have pairs share their answers with the class.

## Conversation 2

Class CD 1, Track 53

1. With books closed, play the recording or read the conversation.

   Young-hee: Did you hear about *The People Next Door*?
   Yumi: No, what happened?
   Young-hee: Well, let me tell you! Brenda caught Stan—that's her boyfriend—kissing another woman.
   Yumi: That's terrible! She should have left him right away!
   Young-hee: She did! She ran out, got in the car, and drove away.
   Yumi: The poor woman! So, where did she go?
   Young-hee: She ended up at the hospital. She was…

   Yumi: Wait a minute. Why did she go to the hospital?
   Young-hee: She was driving too fast and had an accident. Anyway…
   Yumi: She shouldn't have driven so fast. Was she hurt?
   Young-hee: She broke her arm. But listen, the important thing is that she fell in love with the doctor who fixed her arm. Now, as soon as she feels a little better, they're going to start dating.
   Yumi: Let me get this straight. Brenda caught Stan with another woman, got into a car accident, and now she's going out with her doctor?
   Young-hee: That's right.
   Yumi: That's unbelievable. It sounds like a soap opera.
   Young-hee: Yumi. It *is* a soap opera. It's called *The People Next Door*. It's on TV every day at noon.

2. Ask these comprehension questions:

   • *Are they talking about a real situation?* (no)
   • *What is the name of the TV show they are talking about?* (The People Next Door)

3. Say: *Listen again. This time listen for the details of the story.*

4. Play or read the conversation again, pausing for choral repetition. Allow students to write down the information as they listen. Play or read the conversation again, if needed, for students to get all the information.

5. Ask the following questions:

- *Who is Brenda's boyfriend?* (Stan)
- *What did she catch him doing?* (kissing another woman)
- *Where did Brenda go?* (to the hospital)
- *Why?* (She was driving too fast and had an accident.)
- *Who did she fall in love with?* (the doctor who fixed her arm)
- *Who is she going out with now?* (the doctor)

Elicit responses from various students.

## PRONUNCIATION FOCUS
**Class CD 1, Track 54**

1. Explain what the focus is. Play or read the examples in the book and have students repeat chorally.

   **Where did she go?**
   **Was she hurt?**

2. With books open, play or read the conversation again. Tell students to pay attention to the stressed and unstressed words.

3. Paired Reading. Have students practice the conversation, switching roles.

**Student Book page 41**

## Give It a Try

## 1. Saying what someone should have done

### Presentation

1. Have students look at the function box. Give them time to read the examples.

2. Model the exchanges in the function box and have students repeat chorally.

### Practice

**Class CD 1, Track 55**

1. Have students read the directions and look at the pictures.

2. Play or read the example conversation.

   A: Did you hear about Brenda?
   B: No, what happened?
   A: Brenda caught Stan kissing another woman.
   B: She should have left him right away!

3. Discuss what each person should or shouldn't have done. Write students' ideas on the board, if necessary.

4. Pair Work. Have students take turns asking about each person and saying what they should or shouldn't have done.

5. Have pairs demonstrate their exchanges for the class.

## 2. Asking for details

### Presentation

1. Have students look at the function boxes. Give them time to read the examples.

2. Model the exchanges in the function boxes and have students repeat chorally.

### Practice

**Class CD 1, Track 56**

1. Have students read the directions and look at the lists. Go over any vocabulary students don't know.

2. Play or read the example conversation.

   A: Did you hear about Brenda?
   B: No, what happened?
   A: She was driving too fast and had an accident.
   B: Was she hurt?
   A: She broke her arm.

3. Pair Work. Have students decide who will be Student A and who will be Student B. Have students take turns talking about the people on their list and asking for details. Brainstorm possible details and questions about each person and their situation first, if necessary.

4. Have pairs demonstrate their exchanges for the class.

# 3. Interrupting and getting back to the story

## Presentation

1. Have students look at the function box. Give them time to read the examples.

2. Model the exchanges and have students repeat chorally.

## Notes

1. Practice appropriate reactions with students. Model for them the proper intonation and facial expressions for reactions such as *That's weird. Is she OK? Incredible!* etc.

2. Tell students to be careful about how and when they interrupt someone. Explain that interrupting is fine if it is to show concern or to clarify something you didn't understand, but it is impolite to interrupt too often.

## Practice

**Class CD 1, Track 57**

1. Have students read the directions and look at the stories and the word box. Go over any vocabulary students don't know.

2. Play or read the example conversation.

   A: Did you hear about Brenda? She ended up at the hospital. She was…

   B: Wait a minute. Why did she go to the hospital?

   A: She was driving too fast and had an accident. Anyway…

   B: Was she hurt?

   A: She broke her arm. But listen, the important thing is that she fell in love with the doctor who fixed her arm.

   B: Let me get this straight. Brenda caught Stan with another woman, got into a car accident, and now she's going out with her doctor? That's unbelievable.

3. Pair Work. Give students time to choose a story. Brainstorm other story ideas, if necessary. Have students take turns telling a story and interrupting. Practice interrupting a sentence with various students first, if necessary.

4. Have various pairs demonstrate their conversation for the class.

## Extension

Have students use their dictionaries to add words to the **Use These Words** list.

# Listen to This

## Part 1

**Class CD 1, Track 58**

1. Give students time to read the directions and look at the pictures.

2. Tell students to listen to the conversation and number the pictures in the correct order.

3. Play or read the conversations.

   J: Did you hear about what happened to Dave and Meg when they went climbing in the Alps last year?

   S: No, what happened?

   J: They were caught in a sudden snowstorm and got trapped on a narrow ledge. Dave hurt his foot and couldn't climb.

   S: That's terrible! What did they do?

   J: They put up their tent to try and keep warm and have shelter from the snow.

   S: Did they have any food with them?

   J: They just had one chocolate bar.

   S: One chocolate bar? Why didn't they have more food?

   J: Well, they were on their way down and they had eaten almost all of their supplies. Anyway, luckily Meg had her cell phone with her. The signal was very weak, but she managed to call her friend in Geneva and….

   S: In Geneva! Why didn't she phone the emergency services?

   J: Because the signal was too weak, and the batteries were almost dead. But listen, the main thing is, her friend was able to get through to the mountain rescue team, and they sent a helicopter to rescue them.

   S: How long were they trapped there?

   J: Oh, about 16 hours.

   S: That's incredible. They could have frozen to death!

4. Check answers.

**Answers:** 2, 1, 3

## Part 2

1. Give students time to read the directions.

2. Tell students to listen again and write down the questions the woman asks.

3. Play or read the conversation twice.

4. Check answers.

> **Answers:**
> 1. What happened? What did they do? Did they have any food with them? Why didn't they have more food? Why didn't she phone the emergency services? How long were they trapped there?

## Part 3

1. Give students time to read the directions.

2. Play the conversation again, if necessary.

> **Answer:**
> Answers will vary

**Student Book page 43**

## Person to Person

### Part 1

1. Have students read the instructions and look at the pictures.

2. Ask students to describe what is happening in each picture. Write new vocabulary on the board, if necessary.

3. Pair Work. Have students put the pictures in the correct order.

4. Ask several students for their answers.

> **Answers:**
> Order may vary.
> | | |
> |---|---|
> | 1 | 4 or 5 |
> | 3 | 7 |
> | 4 or 5 | 8 |
> | 6 | 2 |

## Part 2

1. Have students read the directions.

2. Pair Work. Have students take turns telling each other the story using the pictures.

3. Have several students tell the story to the class.

## Part 3

1. Have students read the directions.

2. Pair Work. Tell them to discuss what they think the people in the story should have done. Circulate and help as needed.

3. Have pairs report their suggestions to the class. Discuss as a class which suggestions were the most interesting.

## Now Try This

1. Have students read the directions.

2. Give students time to think of a story, real or not, and write it in six sentences. Tell them to cut the sentences into six separate slips of paper.

3. Have pairs swap papers and put the new papers in the correct order and then discuss what the people in the story should have done.

4. Have each pair tell their stories to the class. Ask the other classmates if they can think of anything else the person in the story could have done.

5. Have the class vote on the most interesting story.

## Components

Student Book, pages 44–51, 110
Class CD 1, Tracks 59–69
Optional Activities 6.1–6.2,
page 108

## Objectives

**Functions:** Talking about symptoms, giving, accepting and refusing advice, advising someone *not* to do something, asking for advice, giving and asking about instructions

**Topics:** Illnesses, remedies, prescriptions

**Structures:** Modal verbs *should*, *'d better*, *must*, *could*, *can't*

**Pronunciation Focus:** Unstressed prepositions

**Listen to This:** Listening for specific information: health problems, advice, and pharmacist's recommendations; matching pictures to words mentioned, filling in a chart

---

**Student Book page 44**

## CONSIDER THIS

1. Have students read the text and the questions.

2. Group Work. Divide students into groups of four or five. Have students in each group discuss home remedies they have tried. Help students with vocabulary as needed.

3. Ask volunteers for their answers.

### Vocabulary

Introduce these words and phrases to the students:

*feverish:* red-faced and slightly sweaty

*it didn't do any good:* it didn't help at all

*going around:* spreading from one person to another

*you'd better:* you should

*take your temperature:* use a thermometer to measure your body temperature

### Prelistening

1. Pair Work. Have students open their books and look at the photograph. Have partners describe what they see to each other. Circulate and help with vocabulary as needed.

2. Class Work. Read the title of the conversation and the prelistening question and task. Ask volunteers to answer the question and describe the man's symptoms.

## Conversation 1

**Class CD 1, Track 59**

1. With books closed, play the recording or read the conversation.

Li-wei: You look a little feverish. Are you OK?

Jay: To tell you the truth, I feel terrible.

Li-wei: Why? What's the matter?

Jay: I have a horrible headache and a sore throat.

Li-wei: Did you take anything for it?

Jay: I took some aspirin, but it didn't do any good. I feel awful. My whole body aches.

Li-wei: Why didn't you call the doctor?

Jay: I thought I might feel better after a good night's sleep, but I feel worse this morning.

Li-wei: You know, there's a pretty bad flu going around. Maybe you shouldn't go to class today.

Jay: But I have a test this afternoon!

Li-wei: Why don't you call the doctor and see what she says? You'd better take your temperature first. Then maybe you should lie down.

Jay: That's a good idea. I think I'll lie down for a while.

2. Ask these comprehension questions:

- *How does Speaker 2 feel?* (terrible, sick)
- *What does Speaker 1 think is wrong with him?* (He has the flu.)

3. Play or read the conversation again, pausing for choral repetition.

4. Ask the following questions:
   - *How does Speaker 1 say Speaker 2 looks?* (feverish)
   - *What are Speaker 1's symptoms?* (He has a headache and a sore throat.)
   - *What did he take for it?* (aspirin)
   - *Why didn't he call the doctor?* (He thought he'd feel better after a good night's sleep.)
   - *What does he have this afternoon?* (a test)
   - *What does Speaker 1 advise him to do?* (Call the doctor, take his temperature, and lie down.)

   Elicit responses from various students.

5. Paired Reading. Have students read the conversation, switching roles.

**Student Book page 45**

## Give It a Try

## 1. Talking about symptoms

### *Presentation*

1. Have students look at the function box. Give them time to read the examples.

2. Model the exchanges and have students repeat chorally.

3. Practice a few exchanges with various students.

### Notes

1. Explain that *ache* and *sore* are both used to describe discomfort in an area of the body, but they are not always interchangeable. Tell students to memorize the following:

   *headache, toothache, earache, stomachache, backache,*

   but

   *sore throat, sore elbow, sore knee.*

2. On the board, write:

   *What's the matter?*

   Mark the intonation. Model the intonation and have students repeat.

3. Explain to students that a *splitting headache* is a very bad one that feels like your head is going to split open. Also explain that *pale* means *whitish* and *flushed* means *reddish* or *pinkish*. If time allows, teach students other ways to describe pain or illness such as a *pounding headache, a throbbing pain, a sharp pain, cold and clammy skin, dizzy,* etc.

### *Practice*

**Class CD 1, Track 60**

1. Have students read the directions and look at the list. Go over vocabulary, if necessary.

2. Play or read the example conversation twice.

   A: You look a little feverish. Are you OK?
   B: To tell you the truth, I feel terrible.
   A: Why? What's the matter?
   B: I have a horrible headache and a sore throat.

3. Pair Work. Have students take turns asking and answering questions about four of the situations on the list.

4. Ask several pairs to demonstrate for the class.

## 2. Giving, accepting, and refusing advice

### *Presentation*

1. Have students look at the function box. Give them time to read the examples.

2. Model the exchanges and have students repeat chorally.

3. Practice a few exchanges with various students.

### Note

Explain that *You should...* is a recommendation and *You'd better...* is a strong recommendation.

### *Practice*

**Class CD 1, Track 61**

1. Have students read the directions and look at the list and the words in the box. Go over any vocabulary students don't know.

2. Play or read the example conversation twice.

   A: What's the matter?
   B: I have a horrible headache.
   A: You'd better take some aspirin.
   B: That's a good idea. I'll give it a try.

3. Pair Work. Have students take turns giving, accepting, and refusing advice.

4. Ask several pairs to demonstrate for the class.

### *Extension*

1. Have students use their dictionaries to add words to the **Use These Words** list.

2. Class Discussion. Talk about students' feelings about non-serious illness. For example: if they don't feel well, do they stay home from work or school? Do they like to take medication? Do they go to the doctor often? What is their favorite cold remedy?

## 3. Advising someone *not* to do something

Review. Give a prompt such as *sore throat*. Point to two students and have one of them say that he or she has a sore throat and the other give advice. Continue with other prompts and other pairs.

### Presentation

1. Have students look at the function box. Give them time to read the examples.

2. Model the exchanges and have students repeat chorally.

3. Practice a few exchanges with various students.

### Practice

**Class CD 1, Track 62**

1. Have students read the directions and look at the lists. Go over vocabulary, if necessary.

2. Play or read the example conversation twice.

   A: You look terrible. What's the matter?
   B: I have a horrible headache and a sore throat.
   A: Maybe you shouldn't go to class today.
   B: But I have a test this afternoon!

3. Pair Work. Give students time to think of their own ideas. Have students take turns talking about their symptoms and giving advice.

4. Ask several pairs to demonstrate for the class.

### Extension

Charades. Write various symptoms on pieces of paper. Have a student choose one of the papers and silently act out the symptom. The first student to guess the symptom gives advice to help with that symptom. Continue with other students and symptoms.

## Listen to This

**Class CD 1, Track 63**

Part 1

1. Have students read the directions.

2. Play or read the conversation. Tell students to listen for what is wrong with Jake.

   T: Jake? Are you OK? You look a little pale.
   J: Yeah, I didn't sleep well last night. I had this terrible pain in my knee. I think I strained it when I went cycling yesterday.
   T: Maybe you shouldn't go out today. Why don't you take some aspirin and lie down?
   J: Aspirin makes my stomach feel funny. Do we still have any of the pain relieving gel that I used for my backache?
   T: I'm not sure. I'll have a look. Or why don't you use the heating pad? That really worked well on my back last time.
   J: I suppose so. You used an ice pack, too, didn't you?
   T: Yes, but that didn't really work.
   J: OK. I'll try the heating pad first and then I'll put on some of that gel...if we have any left.

3. Ask volunteers for the answers.

   **Answer:**
   He didn't sleep well because he has a pain in his knee. He thinks he strained his knee.

**Part 2**

1. Have students read the directions.

2. Play or read the conversation again and tell students to listen for which remedies are mentioned. Identify the remedies in the pictures first, if necessary.

3. Play or read the conversation again for students to check their answers.

4. Ask volunteers for the answers.

> **Answers:**
> aspirin, pain relieving gel, heating pad, ice pack

**Part 3**

1. Have students read the directions.

2. Play or read the conversation again and tell students to listen for which remedy Jake chooses.

3. Ask volunteers for the answers.

> **Answers:**
> The heating pad and the pain relieving gel.

**Student Book page 47**

## Let's Talk

**Part 1**

1. Have students read the directions.

2. Give students time to read the list of problems and look at the chart. Go over any vocabulary students don't know.

3. Have students write one of the problems in the chart.

**Note**

Explain to students that when talking to someone they don't know well, it isn't appropriate to talk about personal illness or symptoms. Point out that it is OK to talk about these things with friends, particularly when asking for advice.

**Part 2**

1. Have students read the directions.

2. Give students time to think of a remedy for each of the problems in the chart.

3. Have students walk around the classroom and take turns asking various students for remedies for their problem and offering their remedy for the other students' problems. Make sure they write down the suggested remedies in the chart.

4. Circulate and help as needed.

**Part 3**

1. Have students read the directions.

2. Class Work. Ask students about the remedies they wrote in their charts. Keep track of which ones were the most popular.

# What do you think I should take?

Student Book page 48

## Vocabulary

Introduce these words and phrases to the students:

*non-prescription (medicine)*: (medicine) which can be bought without a doctor's prescription

*tablet*: medicine in a small, round form; pill

*to be allergic to*: to have a bad reaction to (a substance)

*That'll be ($15.50).*: The total cost is ($15.50).

## Prelistening

1.  Have students open their books and look at the photograph. Ask students:

    - *Where are the speakers?* (in a pharmacy)

    - *What do you think the pharmacist is telling the customer?* (how to take a medicine)

2.  Pair Work. Read the title of the conversation and the prelistening question. Have students tell their partners what medicine they take when they have a cold or the flu.

3.  Have pairs share their answers with the class.

## Conversation 2

Class CD 1, Track 64

1.  With books closed, play the recording or read the conversation.

    | | |
    |---|---|
    | Pharmacist: | Can I help you? |
    | Jay: | Hmm…Yes, please. I think I have the flu and I have a big test this afternoon. What do you think I should take? Can you recommend something, please? |
    | Pharmacist: | What are your symptoms? |
    | Jay: | I have a terrible headache, a sore throat, and a fever. |
    | Pharmacist: | That sounds like the flu. You could try a non-prescription pain reliever and fever reducer. Take two tablets every six hours, with food. That should help. If your fever doesn't come down within 24 hours, you should see your doctor. |
    | Jay: | Are there any special instructions? |
    | Pharmacist: | Yes, you must take these with food. And you can't drink any alcohol. Are you allergic to aspirin? |
    | Jay: | No, I'm not. |
    | Pharmacist: | You'll be fine then. |
    | Jay: | OK, I'll take those and a package of cough drops, please. |
    | Pharmacist: | That'll be $15.50. |

2.  Ask these comprehension questions:

    - *What is Speaker 2's problem?* (He has the flu.)
    - *What does he have to do this afternoon?* (take a test)

3.  Say: *Listen again. This time listen for the pharmacist's advice.*

4.  Play or read the conversation again, pausing for choral repetition. Allow students to write down the information as they listen. Play or read the conversation again, if needed, for students to get all the information.

5.  Ask the following questions:

    - *What medicine does the pharmacist recommend?* (a non-prescription pain reliever and fever reducer)
    - *How does she say to take the medicine?* (two tablets every six hours, with food)
    - *When should Speaker 2 see his doctor?* (if his fever doesn't come down within 24 hours)
    - *What else does Speaker 2 buy?* (cough drops)
    - *What is the total cost of the medicine?* ($15.50)

    Elicit responses from various students.

## PRONUNCIATION FOCUS

Class CD 1, Track 65

1.  Explain what the focus is. Play or read the examples in the book and have students repeat chorally.

    allergic to aspirin
    a package of cough drops

2.  With books open, play or read the conversation again. Tell students to pay attention to the pronunciation of the prepositions.

3.  Paired Reading. Have students practice the conversation, switching roles.

## Give It a Try

## 1. Asking for advice

### Presentation

1. Have students look at the function box. Give them time to read the examples.

2. Model the exchange and have students repeat chorally.

3. Have a few pairs model the exchanges with different combinations for the class.

### Practice

**Class CD 1, Track 66**

1. Have students read the directions and look at the list and the words in the box. Go over vocabulary, if necessary.

2. Give students time to write their own ideas about a cause for discomfort or illness.

3. Play or read the example conversation.

   A: What do you think I should take for a headache?
   B: You could try this pain reliever.

4. Pair Work. Have students take turns talking about a problem and giving advice.

5. Have pairs demonstrate their exchanges for the class.

### Extension

Have students use their dictionaries to add words to the **Use These Words** list.

## 2. Giving instructions

### Presentation

1. Have students look at the function box. Give them time to read the examples.

2. Model the exchange and have students repeat chorally.

### Practice

**Class CD 1, Track 67**

1. Have students read the directions.

2. Play or read the example conversation.

   A: I have a terrible headache and a fever. What do you think I should take?
   B: You could try this fever reducer.
   A: How often do I have to take it?
   B: Take two tablets every six hours with food. Your fever should come down within 24 hours.

3. Pair Work. Have students decide who will be Student A and who will be Student B. Have students take turns asking a pharmacist about their problem and telling the customer how to take the medicine. Review the problems from the previous practice, if necessary.

4. Have pairs demonstrate their exchanges for the class.

## 3. Asking about instructions

### Presentation

1. Have students look at the function boxes. Give them time to read the examples.

2. Model the examples and have students repeat chorally.

### Note
Remind students that the content words in a sentence are stressed. On the board write the following sentences without marking the stressed words:

*Do not touch your eyes with this.*

*Shake the bottle first.*

*Don't sit out in the sun.*

*Take this with a meal.*

Have volunteers come up and mark the content words in each sentence. Model each sentence and have students repeat.

**Student Book page 50**

### Practice 1

1. Have students read the directions for the activity and look at the labels and the list of instructions. Go over any vocabulary students don't know.

2. Read the list of instructions. Ask students what kind of medicine would have these instructions, and why that medicine has those specific instructions.

3. Pair Work. Have students match the labels with the instructions.

4. Ask various students for the answers.

## Practice 2

Class CD 1, Track 68

1. Have students read the directions for the activity.

2. Play or read the example conversation.

   A: Are there any special instructions?
   B: You must take these with food.
   A: Am I allowed to take aspirin with this medication?
   B: No, you shouldn't take any aspirin.

3. Pair Work. Have students take turns asking and answering questions about the medicines in Practice 1.

4. Have pairs demonstrate their exchanges for the class.

## Practice 3

1. Have students read the directions for the activity.

2. Give students time to think of three medicines and any special instructions for them.

3. Pair Work. Have students talk about what you must and must not do with the medicines they chose. Circulate and help as needed.

4. Have various pairs report their discussion to the class.

## Listen to This

Class CD 1, Track 69

### Part 1

1. Give students time to read the directions and look at the chart.

2. Tell students to listen to the conversations and write down the problem in each case.

3. Play or read the conversations.

   **1**
   P: Good morning. What can I do for you?
   C: Oh, this is embarrassing….
   P: Don't worry. How can I help?
   C: I'm looking for something for pimples. What do you recommend?
   P: This cream is very good. Use it every morning and evening after washing your face.
   C: Should I use a lot or just a little?
   P: Just a little, otherwise your skin will dry out.
   C: OK. I'll take it. Thanks.

   **2**
   C: Excuse me. Can you help me?
   P: Certainly.
   C: I wonder if you have anything for backaches.
   P: This ointment is very good.
   C: I've used that. It didn't really help. The thing is, I sit at the computer about ten hours a day. I think that's the problem.
   P: One of these might help.
   C: What is it?
   P: It's a back-support cushion.
   C: Are there any special instructions?
   P: Try not to lean forward when you work. Sit with your back straight so that your knees, hips, and elbows form right angles. And take frequent breaks to stretch your muscles.
   C: OK. I'll give it a try. Thanks a lot.

   **3**
   P: Is there something I can help you with, ma'am?
   C: Yes, please! I really need something for this sunburn.
   P: Too much sun is dangerous, you know.
   C: I know, but I fell asleep at the beach.
   P: Try this sunburn lotion. It'll help the pain. It's also got a moisturizer in it.
   C: How often do I put this on?
   P: Every two hours, until the pain subsides.
   C: Is there anything else I can do?
   P: Well, you could try soaking in a cool bath for twenty minutes before putting the lotion on your skin.
   C: Thanks a lot.

4. Check answers.

**Answers:**
1. pimples
2. backache
3. sunburn

## Part 2

1. Give students time to read the directions.

2. Tell students to listen again and write down what each customer buys.

3. Play or read the conversations.

4. Check answers.

**Answers:**
1. a cream
2. a back-support cushion
3. sunburn lotion

## Part 3

1. Give students time to read the directions.

2. Tell students to listen again for the instructions from the pharmacist.

3. Play or read the conversations.

4. Check answers.

**Answers:**
1. Use only a little every morning and evening, after washing your face.
2. Try not to lean forward when you work. Sit with your back straight so that your knees, hips, and elbows form right angles. Take frequent breaks to stretch your muscles.
3. Put the lotion on every 2 hours until the pain subsides. Soak in a cool bath for 20 minutes before putting on the lotion.

**Student Book pages 51 & 110**

## Person to Person

### Part 1

1. Divide the class into pairs and have students decide who will be Student A and who will be Student B. Remind Student B to look at page 110.

2. Have students read the directions and look at the pictures.

3. To check comprehension, ask:

   Student B, *what is your problem?* (insomnia)

   Student A, *what will you do?* (recommend a remedy and give special instructions)

   Brainstorm possible remedies and special instructions for remedies, if necessary.

4. Pair Work. Have students discuss the problem and the remedy.

5. Ask several pairs to demonstrate for the class.

### Part 2

1. Have students read the directions.

2. To check comprehension, ask:

   Student A, *what is your problem?* (migraines)

   Student B, *what will you do?* (recommend a remedy and give special instructions)

   Brainstorm possible remedies and special instructions for remedies, if necessary.

3. Pair Work. Have students discuss the problem and the remedy.

4. Have several pairs demonstrate for the class.

### Part 3

1. Divide Students A and B into separate groups.

2. Have students read the directions.

3. Group Work. Have students tell the remedies they chose for each problem. Tell each group to discuss the remedies and say which was the most popular.

4. Have groups report their discussions to the class. Discuss as a class which suggestions were the most interesting.

### *Extension*

Class Discussion. Discuss with students their favorite remedy for the hiccups. Vote on who has the most unusual remedy.

## Now Try This

1. Have students read the directions.

2. Give students time to think of a common health problem.

3. Pair Work. Have students take turns talking about a health problem and possible remedies.

4. Have pairs report their discussion to the class. Have the class vote on the most interesting remedy.

# Review:
## Units 4–6

## Components
Student Book, pages 52–53
Class CD 1, tracks 70–72

## Listen To This Unit 4

**Class CD 1, Track 70**

1. Have students read the directions and look at the picture and the chart.

2. Play or read the talk.

> Today I'm going to talk to you about the problem of increasing traffic in our cities. First, I will describe some of the effects caused by too many cars in our cities. Then I will suggest a few possible solutions.
>
> What are some of the effects caused by too many cars in our cities?
>
> First, cars use a lot of space. Think of all the space needed for parking and driving, and think what a difference it would make if it were used instead for parks, trees, and recreation areas.
>
> Second, cars create a lot of air and noise pollution. Our cities are getting dirtier and noisier and more unhealthy every day. Just think how much healthier we would be if there were fewer cars.
>
> Third, cars are dangerous. Cars cause hundreds of accidents, injuries, and deaths in our cities every year.
>
> Well, you are going to ask, what can we do about it? We can't forbid people to buy or use their cars, can we?
>
> There are a number of solutions available that have been tried in various cities around the world.
>
> One is to create pedestrian or car-free zones. At least there will be some areas of the city where people can walk in peace and safety.
>
> Another solution is to charge private cars for entering the city and increase parking fees. If it becomes cheaper to use public transportation, people will avoid using their cars unless it is really necessary.
>
> A third way is to encourage people to use public transportation by improving public transportation services, offering special discounts and reasonable prices so that buses and trains are cheaper and more convenient.
>
> Now, if you have any questions....

3. Have students fill out the chart.

4. Play or read the talk again for students to check their answers.

5. Ask volunteers for the answers.

**Answers:**
Effects:
1. Cars use a lot of space.
2. Cars create air and noise pollution.
3. Cars are dangerous.
Solutions:
1. create car-free zones
2. charge cars to enter the city and increase parking fees
3. encourage people to use public transportation

## Give It a Try

1. Have students read the directions and look at the problems.

2. Group Work. Give students time to choose one problem from the list and think of one of their own. Have one student tell the group his or her problem and the other students in the group give advice. The person who gives the best advice gets a point. Continue with other students and problems.

3. Have the student with the most points tell the class the advice he or she gave.

## Listen To This Unit 5

**Class CD 1, Track 71**

1. Have students read the directions and look at the chart.

2. Play or read the conversations.

> **1**
> W: Did I tell you about Dave and Atsuko?
> M: No. What?
> W: They're going to get married!
> M: That's great news!
> W: You know Dave's been asking her to marry him for quite a long time and she finally said yes!
> M: So when's the wedding?
> W: Next month.

**2**

W: How's Debbie doing these days?
M: Oh, didn't you hear about her new job? She's going to teach English in Italy.
W: Oh, that's fantastic! When will she be leaving?
M: In August.
W: I bet she's really excited about that.

**3**

M: Have you heard about what happened to Marco on vacation?
W: No, what happened?
M: He was on vacation in Australia, when someone broke into his hotel room and stole all his money and his passport.
W: That's terrible! What did he do?
M: Fortunately, he had a photocopy of his passport, which he kept separately. He took that to the embassy and they managed to get him another passport within a few days.
W: That was lucky!

3. Have students fill out the chart with the names of the people mentioned in the conversation, what happened to them, and if that was good or bad news.

4. Ask volunteers for the answers.

> **Answers:**
> 1. Dave and Atsuko; they're getting married; good
> 2. Debbie; she has a new job teaching English in Italy; good
> 3. Marco; he was robbed on vacation in Australia; bad

**Student Book page 53**

## Give It a Try

1. Have students read the directions and look at the headlines.

2. Group Work. Divide the class into groups of four. Give students time to choose a headline and think of the details of the story. Have each person in the group take turns telling the story and answering questions from the group. Have the group discuss what the person in the story should have done.

3. Have a student from each group tell their story to the class.

## Listen To This Unit 6

Class CD 1, Track 72

1. Have students read the directions and look at the chart.

2. Play or read the conversation.

T: What's the matter, Shami? You're not walking too well.
S: Oh, Tom. I have this terrible pain in my knee.
T: I'm sorry to hear that.
S: My knee has swollen up, and it's really bad when I go up and down the stairs like this.
T: Have you been to the doctor?
S: Yes, she said I should rest and she gave me some painkillers.
T: Have you tried anything else?
S: Well, my friend lent me a heating pad, and I tried that for a while, but it had no effect at all.
T: What about ice packs?
S: No. I haven't tried that yet. That's a good idea.
T: Also, there's a really good cream you can get from the pharmacy. When you rub it on your muscles, it makes the joints feel warm and it relieves some of the pain, too.
S: That sounds good. What's the name of it? I'll go and get some right away.
T: Hang on a minute. I'll write down the name for you.

3. Have students fill out the chart.

4. Play or read the conversation again for students to check their answers.

5. Ask volunteers for the answers.

> **Answers:**
> Symptoms: terrible pain in her knee, swollen knee
> Remedies Shami has tried: painkillers, heating pad
> Remedies Shami hasn't tried: ice packs, heat cream

## Give It a Try

1. Have students read the directions and look at the pictures.

2. Pair Work. Give students time to write questions to ask about each item. Have students take turns asking and answering questions about how to use each item.

3. Have pairs demonstrate their conversations for the class.

# Unit 7
# What's this thing?

## Components

Student Book, pages 54–61
Class CD 2, Tracks 2–11
Optional Activities 7.1–7.2,
pages 108–109

## Objectives

**Functions:** Describing what objects are used for, giving instructions, discussing needs and requirements, asking for clarification, talking about consequences

**Topics:** Kitchen utensils, recipes, outdoor activities and equipment

**Structures:** *Used/be for* + gerund, *used/be to* + base form, sequence adverbs, imperative (with *you*)

**Pronunciation Focus:** Blending of final [t] of a word with initial consonant of next word

**Listen to This:** Listening for specific information: ingredients and instructions in recipes, necessary items for activities; filling in charts

---

Student Book page 54

## CONSIDER THIS

1. Have students read the text and the question.
2. Group Work. Divide students into groups of four or five. Have students in each group discuss if they have ever bought or sold anything on-line. Help students with vocabulary as needed.
3. Ask volunteers for their answers.

### Vocabulary

Introduce these words and phrases to the students:

*clean out:* clean completely

*throw out:* throw away as garbage

*keep adding:* continue adding

*homemade:* made at home, not manufactured

### Prelistening

1. Pair Work. Have students open their books and look at the photograph. Have partners describe what they see to each other. Circulate and help with vocabulary as needed.
2. Class Work. Read the title of the conversation and the prelistening question. Ask volunteers to answer the question.

## Conversation 1

Class CD 2, Track 2

1. With books closed, play the recording or read the conversation.

   Denise: Thanks for helping me clean out the garage.
   Terumi: I'm glad to do it. It's interesting.
   Denise: Wow! The people in my family are real collectors! They never throw anything out.
   Terumi: You're not kidding. What's this thing?
   Denise: It's an old ice-cream maker, I think.
   Terumi: How do you use it?
   Denise: Let's see if I can remember…oh, yeah. First, you put this metal container in the bottom of the tub. Then you fill it with ice-cream mixture made from eggs, sugar, and milk. Next, you put the lid on the metal container and fill the rest of the tub with ice and salt.
   Terumi: What's next?
   Denise: After that, you turn this handle, and you keep adding salt and ice until you can't turn the handle any more.
   Terumi: And then what?
   Denise: You open it up, and there's your delicious homemade ice cream.

2. Ask these comprehension questions:
   • *Where are the speakers?* (a garage)
   • *What do you think she is holding?* (ice cream maker; answers may vary)

3. Play or read the conversation again, pausing for choral repetition.

4. Ask the following questions:
   - *What are they doing?* (cleaning out the garage)
   - *Why does Speaker 1 call her family "collectors?"* (Because they never throw anything out.)
   - *What do they find?* (an old ice-cream maker)
   - *What do you do first to make ice cream?* (Put the metal container in the bottom of the tub.)
   - *What's next?* (Put in the ice-cream mixture.)
   - *What's after that?* (Close the container and fill in the tub with ice and salt, then turn the handle and keep adding ice and salt until you can't turn the handle any more.)

   Elicit responses from various students.

5. Paired Reading. Have students read the conversation, switching roles.

**Student Book page 55**

## Give It a Try

## 1. Describing what objects are used for

### Presentation

1. Have students look at the function boxes. Give them time to read the examples.

2. Model the exchanges and have students repeat chorally.

3. Practice a few exchanges with various students.

### Notes

1. Point out that the phrase *It's used for* is followed by the gerund *making*. The phrase *It's used to* is followed by the base form *make*. Both phrases have the same meaning.

2. Explain to students that many people in the United States store old furniture, clothes, pictures, etc. in their garages and their attics. Sometimes, when those places get too full, the person will have a "garage sale" or "yard sale," which means they will sell all the things they don't want anymore for a very low price. The sale is held in the garage or the front yard.

### Practice 1

Class CD 2, Track 3

1. Have students read the directions and look at the pictures, the captions, and the list. Go over vocabulary, if necessary.

2. Play or read the example conversation twice.

   A: What's this thing used for?
   B: It's used for making ice cream.

3. Pair Work. Have students take turns asking and answering questions about one of the items pictured.

4. Ask several pairs to demonstrate for the class.

### Practice 2

1. Have students read the directions for the activity and look at the words in the box. Go over any words students don't know.

2. Give students time to think of a kitchen item that they use and how to describe it.

3. Group Work. Have students take turns describing a kitchen item and guessing what it is.

4. Have each group pick the most unusual item in their group and describe it for the class to guess what it is.

### Extension

1. Bring in magazine pictures of other tools and appliances. Hold up each picture and have students describe how it is used.

2. Have students use their dictionaries to add words to the **Use These Words** list.

## 2. Giving instructions

### Presentation

1.  Have students look at the function box. Give them time to read the examples.

2.  Model the exchanges and have students repeat chorally.

3.  Practice a few exchanges with various students.

### Note
Review the time sequence expressions *first, second, then, next, after that, finally.*

### Practice 1

Class CD 2, Track 4

Have students read the directions. Review the objects from Practice 1 in Part 1, if necessary.

1.  Play or read the example conversation twice.

    A: What's this thing?
    B: It's an ice-cream maker.
    A: How do you use it?
    B: First, you put this metal container in the bottom of the tub....

2.  Pair Work. Have students take turns explaining how the objects work. Discuss as a class how each object works first, if necessary.

3.  Ask several pairs to demonstrate for the class.

### Practice 2

1.  Have students read the directions and look at the pictures and the list of instructions to make an omelette. Go over any vocabulary students don't know.

2.  Give students time to number the instructions in the correct order.

3.  Pair Work. Have students take turns explaining how to make an omelette. Make sure they use sequence time expressions.

4.  Ask several pairs to demonstrate for the class.

### Extension

Write the steps to three different types of activities (making coffee, painting a room, doing laundry, etc.) on slips of paper, with each step on a separate slip. Make enough copies so that each group of students has a scrambled set of slips for the three activities. Give all the slips to each group and have them figure out which steps go together and then put the steps for all three activities in the correct order.

## Listen to This

Class CD 2, Track 5

### Note
You may need to review or introduce recipe measurements such as *tablespoon, pinch, medium,* etc., and some kitchen utensils such as *spatula, knife, grater.*

### Part 1

1.  Have students read the directions and look at the chart.

2.  Play or read the recipe. Tell students to listen for what the ingredients are and write them in the chart. Play or read it again, if necessary.

    Here's a quick and easy recipe for potato pancakes. Delicious as an appetizer or as a main course!
    First, the ingredients. You'll need six medium potatoes, two eggs, two tablespoons of flour, one small onion, some vegetable oil, and a pinch of salt and pepper.
    Now here's how to make them. First, grate the potatoes and squeeze them dry. Next, chop the onion. After that, mix together the eggs, flour, salt, and pepper. Then mix in the potatoes and the onion.
    Finally, heat the oil in a frying pan, drop the potato mixture into the pan in small spoonfuls, and cook for three minutes on each side until they are brown and crisp.
    Serve with applesauce and sour cream. That's it! Easy!

3.  Ask volunteers for the answers.

> **Answer:**
> 6 medium potatoes, 2 eggs, 2 tablespoons of flour, one small onion, some vegetable oil, a pinch of salt and pepper

## Part 2

1. Have students read the directions.

2. Play or read the conversation again and tell students to listen for the instructions this time.

3. Play or read the talk again for students to check their answers.

4. Ask volunteers for their answers.

**Answers:**
1. grate the potatoes and squeeze them dry
2. chop the onion
3. mix together the eggs, flour, salt, and pepper
4. mix in the potatoes and the onion
5. heat the oil
6. drop small spoonfuls of the mixture into the frying pan
7. cook for three minutes on each side

## Part 3

1. Have students read the directions.

2. Tell students to listen again for what tools they need.

3. Ask volunteers for their answers.

**Possible Answers:**
grater, knife, spoon, measuring spoon, bowl, frying pan, spatula, stove

## Let's Talk

### Part 1

1. Have students read the directions and look at the pictures and the captions.

2. Give students time to think of how to pantomime using one of the items.

3. Group Work. Have students take turns pantomiming using the item and guessing what it is.

### Part 2

1. Have students read the directions.

2. Give students time to choose one item and think of how to explain using it.

3. Pair Work. Have students take turns explaining how to use one of the items.

4. Have several pairs demonstrate for the class.

### Part 3

1. Have students read the directions.

2. Give students time to think of a different item and how to pantomime using it.

3. Pair Work. Have students take turns pantomiming and guessing.

4. Have several students pantomime their items for the whole class in a game of charades.

# What else do I need?

## Vocabulary

Introduce these words and phrases to the students:

*barbecue:* an outdoor party where food gets cooked on a metal rack directly over flames

*sunscreen:* a lotion that you put on your skin to protect it from the sun

*insect repellent:* a substance used to keep insects away

*mosquito:* a small flying insect that bites

*cooler:* container, usually a portable box, to keep food and drinks cool

*charcoal:* black burned wood, usually used as fuel in barbecues

*fire extinguisher:* a cylindrical container that shoots out foam to put out fires

## Prelistening

1. Have students open their books and look at the photograph. Ask:

   - *Where are the speakers?* (in front of a garage)
   - *What were they doing before?* (cleaning out the garage)

2. Pair Work. Read the title of the conversation and the prelistening questions. Have students discuss with their partners if they have picnics and what do they usually take to them.

3. Have pairs share their answers with the class.

## Conversation 2

Class CD 2, Track 6

1. With books closed, play the recording or read the conversation.

   Denise: Hey, Terumi, would you like to go to the beach for a barbie with us next weekend?

   Terumi: A barbie, what's that?

   Denise: It's a barbecue! We'll cook food for everyone at the beach. Look, our outdoor grill is right here.

   Terumi: I'd love to come. Do I need to bring anything?

   Denise: Well, you need a hat and some sunscreen. You could get badly sunburned out there! You might also need some insect repellent.

   Terumi: What do I need insect repellent for?

   Denise: It's to keep mosquitoes and other insects away. They're attracted by the smell of the food.

   Terumi: OK. What else do I need?

   Denise: That's it, really. But we'll also be taking an esky.

   Terumi: What's an esky?

   Denise: It's for keeping drinks cool!

   Terumi: Oh, a cooler!

   Denise: Yeah! And some charcoal, here it is...oh, yes, and a fire extinguisher! Just in case!

2. Ask these comprehension questions:

   - *What will Speaker 1 do next weekend?* (go to the beach for a barbecue)
   - *Will Speaker 2 go to the barbecue?* (yes)

3. Say: *Listen again. This time listen for what they need to take to the barbecue.*

4. Play or read the conversation again, pausing for choral repetition. Allow students to write down the information as they listen. Play or read the conversation again, if needed, for students to get all the information.

5. Ask the following questions:

   - *What will Speaker 2 need to bring?* (hat, sunscreen, insect repellent)
   - *What else will they bring?* (barbecue grill, cooler, charcoal, fire extinguisher)
   - *What's the American word for "esky?"* (cooler)

   Elicit responses from various students.

## PRONUNCIATION FOCUS

Class CD 2, Track 7

1. Explain what the focus is. Play or read the examples in the book and have students repeat chorally.

   next weekend
   get sunburned
   insect repellent
   That's it, really.

2. With books open, play or read the conversation again. Tell students to pay attention to the linked words.

3. Paired Reading. Have students practice the conversation, switching roles.

## Extension

Class Discussion. Ask students if they ever throw big parties, either for the holidays or during the weekend or vacations. Discuss how they prepare for it and the kinds of things they need.

**Student Book page 59**

## Give It a Try

## 1. Discussing needs and requirements

### Presentation

1. Have students look at the function box. Give them time to read the examples.

2. Model the exchanges and have students repeat chorally.

### Extension

Write three or four different types of events or trips on the board such as a trip to the Amazon, attending the Academy Awards, buying new furniture for a new apartment, etc. Discuss with students the types of things they need to take into consideration when deciding what they need for each event. Ask students to say what they would bring for each event and write them on the board.

### Practice

**Class CD 2, Track 8**

1. Have students read the directions and look at the list and the words in the box. Go over any vocabulary students don't know.

2. Play or read the example conversation twice.

   A: Would you like to go to the beach for a barbie with us next weekend?
   B: I'd love to come. Do I need to bring anything?
   A: Yes, you need a hat.
   B: What else do I need?
   A: That's it.

3. Give students time to write their own ideas about an event or trip. Brainstorm things to bring to each event on the list first, if necessary.

4. Pair Work. Have students take turns inviting their partner somewhere and saying what they should bring.

5. Have pairs demonstrate their exchanges for the class.

### Extension

Have students use their dictionaries to add words to the **Use These Words** list.

## 2. Asking for clarification

### Presentation

1. Have students look at the function boxes. Give them time to read the examples.

2. Model the exchanges and have students repeat chorally.

### Practice 1

**Class CD 2, Track 9**

1. Have students read the directions.

2. Play or read the example conversation twice.

   A: What do I need insect repellent for?
   B: It's to keep mosquitoes and other insects away.

3. Pair Work. Have students take turns asking why they need to bring each item from their discussion in Part 1.

4. Have pairs demonstrate their exchanges for the class.

### Practice 2

1. Have students read the directions.

2. Pair Work. Have students take turns asking their partner to a birthday party and asking what to bring.

3. Have pairs demonstrate their exchanges for the class.

### Extension

Have students think of an event and write down a list of things that they will need for it. Have them read their list to members of their group and have the group guess what the event is. Then have students say why each item is needed.

# 3. Talking about consequences

## Presentation

1. Have students look at the function boxes. Give them time to read the examples.

2. Model the exchanges and have students repeat chorally.

## Practice 1

**Class CD 2, Track 10**

1. Have students read the directions.

2. Play or read the example conversation twice.

   A: Do I need to bring anything?
   B: Yes, you need a hat.
   A: Why do I need a hat?
   B: If you don't wear a hat, you'll get sunburned.

3. Brainstorm with students the kinds of things they would need to take on a trip to Australia. Talk about the kinds of things that someone would do on a trip to Australia and what they would need to bring to avoid negative consequences.

4. Pair Work. Have students decide who will be Student A and who will be Student B. Have Student A suggest things for Student B to bring to Australia and why they need each item.

5. Have pairs demonstrate their conversation for the class.

## Practice 2

1. Have students read the directions.

2. Brainstorm with students the kinds of things they would need to take on a trip to Alaska. Talk about the kinds of things that someone would do on a trip to Alaska and what they would need to bring to avoid negative consequences.

3. Pair Work. Have Student B suggest things for Student A to bring to Alaska and why they need each item.

4. Have pairs demonstrate their conversation for the class.

## Listen to This

### Part 1

**Class CD 2, Track 11**

1. Give students time to read the directions and look at the chart.

2. Tell students to listen to the conversation and write the activities that Heidi and Nicki are going to do.

3. Play or read the conversation.

   H: Hi, Nicki! So, are you ready for my visit?
   N: Yup! How about you? Are you ready to visit me?
   H: I've got my skis, ski poles, and boots for skiing. What else?
   N: You should have a pair of strong sunglasses to protect your eyes. The snow gets awfully bright. Did you pack any shorts?
   H: Shorts! What do I need shorts for? I'm going there to ski.
   N: I know. I thought you might want to wear them on really warm sunny days. And how could I forget? Sunscreen!
   H: I know…for the sun, right?
   N: Right. But really, bring some so you don't get a sunburn. Are you bringing a nice dress or anything?
   H: Do I need one?
   N: Bring one—but not too fancy—in case we all go out for a nice dinner one night.
   H: OK. What else?
   N: Bring lots of comfortable clothes for relaxing in.
   H: Great idea. I'm looking forward to sitting around in front of the fire after a day of skiing.

4. Check answers.

> **Answers:**
> skiing, go out to dinner, sitting in front of the fire

### Part 2

1. Give students time to read the directions.

2. Tell students to listen again and write down the items that Heidi needs to bring to Aspen.

3. Play or read the conversation.

4. Check answers.

> **Answers:**
> skis, ski poles, ski boots; sunglasses, sunscreen, shorts, a nice dress; comfortable warm clothes

## Part 3

1. Give students time to read the directions.

2. Tell students to listen again for the reasons why Heidi needs to bring each item.

3. Play or read the conversation.

4. Check answers.

> **Answer:**
> skis, ski poles, ski boots for skiing;
> sunglasses, sunscreen for the bright sun;
> shorts for warm days;
> a nice dress for a nice dinner at a restaurant;
> comfortable warm clothes for relaxing

**Student Book page 61**

## Person to Person

### Part 1

1. Have students read the instructions and look at the pictures around the chart.

2. Ask students what each item is and when, how, or why it is used.

3. Give students time to choose a topic.

4. Have them list the tools they will need and make a list of steps for how to make it.

5. Circulate and help as needed.

### Part 2

1. Have students read the directions.

2. Pair Work. Have Student A tell Student B the tools they need for making their item and give the instructions. Make sure Student B asks questions about the tools and the instructions and takes notes.

3. Circulate and help as needed.

### Part 3

1. Have students read the directions.

2. Pair Work. Have students switch roles so that Student B tells Student A the tools they need and the instructions for making their item. Make sure Student A asks questions about the tools and instructions and takes notes.

3. Circulate and help as needed.

## Now Try This

1. Have students read the directions.

2. Give students time to think of how to pantomime each step of their partner's item. Tell them to use their notes.

3. Have a student pantomime the process of making their partner's item. Tell the class to guess what is happening in each step.

4. Once students have guessed each step, have them guess what was being made.

5. Continue with other students.

# We'd like to book a hotel.

## Components

Student Book, pages 62–69, 111
Class CD 2, Tracks 12–22
Optional Activities 8.1–8.2,
page 109

## Objectives

**Functions:** Asking about types of hotels, asking for details, making a reservation, checking in, making requests, asking about hotel services

**Topics:** Hotels, reservations, services

**Structures:** Requests, Yes/No questions, embedded questions

**Pronunciation Focus:** Unstressed form of *can*

**Listen to This:** Listening for specific information: hotel requests; filling in a form, filling in a chart

---

**Student Book page 62**

## CONSIDER THIS

1. Have students read the text and the question. Help with any words students don't know.

2. Class Work. Have several students answer if they would like to stay in Jules' Undersea Lodge and why.

### Vocabulary

Introduce these words and phrases to the students:

*a package:* the parts of a vacation that a travel agent can put together for a customer, usually including plane ticket, car rental, and hotel reservation

*budget hotel:* an inexpensive hotel

*luxury resort:* a very expensive hotel that usually includes facilities such as a swimming pool, sports areas, a spa, etc.

*in the middle:* not too expensive and not too cheap

*brochure:* information pamphlet

*reserve:* to book (a room)

### Prelistening

1. Pair Work. Have students open their books and look at the photograph. Have partners describe what they see to each other. Circulate and help with vocabulary as needed.

2. Class Work. Read the title of the conversation and the prelistening question and task. Ask volunteers to answer the questions.

## Conversation 1

**Class CD 2, Track 12**

1. With books closed, play the recording or read the conversation.

   Agent: Can I help you?
   Julie: We'd like to book a hotel in Tioman for one week.
   Agent: Are you interested in a hotel or a package?
   Lisa: Well, we'd like to learn how to scuba dive, so the package would be better, I think.
   Agent: I see. Do you want to stay in a budget hotel or a luxury resort?
   Julie: Mm, something in the middle, I think.
   Agent: OK. Take a look at this brochure.
   Julie: Where is this hotel?
   Agent: Oh, it's right on the beach.
   Lisa: This looks perfect. We'd like to reserve a double room from September 23-30.
   Agent: Certainly. I just need your names, please.

2. Ask these comprehension questions:

   • *Where are the speakers?* (in a travel agency)
   • *Do they want to book a ticket or a hotel?* (a hotel)
   • *Where?* (in Tioman)

3. Play or read the conversation again, pausing for choral repetition.

4. Ask the following questions:
   - *How long do they want to stay in Tioman?* (one week)
   - *What do they want to do there?* (learn to scuba dive)
   - *Where is the hotel located?* (on the beach)
   - *What days do they want to book the room for?* (September 23 to 30)

   Elicit responses from various students.

5. Paired Reading. Have students read the conversation, switching roles.

**Student Book page 63**

## Give It a Try

## 1. Asking about types of hotels

### Presentation

1. Have students look at the function box. Give them time to read the examples.

2. Model the exchanges and have students repeat chorally.

3. Practice a few exchanges with various students.

### Practice

**Class CD 2, Track 13**

1. Have students read the directions and look at the hotel descriptions. Go over vocabulary, if necessary.

2. Play or read the example conversation twice.

   A: We'd like to book a hotel in Tioman, please.
   B: Are you interested in a hotel or a package?
   A: Well, a package would be better.
   B: Take a look at this brochure.
   A: This looks perfect.

3. Pair Work. Have students take turns asking and answering questions about the hotels pictured.

4. Ask several pairs to demonstrate for the class.

### Note
Make sure students understand the different kinds of rooms in a hotel. A *double room* sleeps two people and can have two single beds, two full beds, or one full or queen bed. A *suite* can have a bedroom, a living room, and a small kitchen.

## 2. Asking for details

### Presentation

1. Have students look at the function box. Give them time to read the examples.

2. Model the exchanges and have students repeat chorally.

3. Practice a few exchanges with various students.

### Practice

**Class CD 2, Track 14**

1. Have students read the directions and look at the list and the words in the box. Go over any words students don't know.

2. Play or read the example conversation twice.

   A: Where is the Spa Resort Hotel?
   B: It's on the beach.
   A: Does it have a swimming pool?
   B: Yes, it does.

3. Pair Work. Have students take turns asking and answering questions about two of the hotels in Part 1. Brainstorm possible questions and answers for some of the things on the list first, if necessary.

### Extension

1. Class Discussion. Discuss with the class what types of hotels they usually stay in when they travel. Ask them to describe their ideal hotel.

2. Divide the class into groups. Have each group design a brochure for a hotel. Tell them the brochure must include the location, prices for types of rooms, facilities, and special features of the hotel.

3. Have students use their dictionaries to add words to the **Use These Words** list.

# 3. Making a reservation

## *Presentation*

1. Have students look at the function box. Give them time to read the examples.

2. Model the exchanges and have students repeat chorally.

3. Practice a few exchanges with various students.

## *Practice*

**Class CD 2, Track 15**

1. Have students read the directions. Review the hotels from the Practice in Part 1, if necessary.

2. Play or read the example conversation twice.

   A: I'd like to reserve a double room at the Spa Resort Hotel, please.
   B: Certainly. For what dates?
   A: From September 23–30.
   B: Could I have your name, please?
   A: Yes, my last name is Park. P-a-r-k.

3. Pair Work. Have students take turns being a tourist and a travel agent and making reservations for the hotels in the Practice in Part 1.

4. Ask several pairs to demonstrate for the class.

## Listen to This

**Class CD 2, Track 16**

Part 1

1. Have students read the directions and look at the list.

2. Play or read the conversation. Tell students to listen for what kind of information is mentioned. Play or read the conversation again, if necessary.

   C:      Palm Tree Hotel. How can I help you?
   Ms. G:  Oh, hello. Could you tell me if you have any rooms free for Thursday and Friday next week?
   C:      For how many people?
   Ms. G:  A single room, please.
   C:      Yes, we have a single room available, that's no problem.
   Ms. G:  OK, I'd like to make a reservation please. The name is Gardiner. G-a-r-d-i-n-e-r. Ms. Emily Gardiner. And it's for two nights from June 28–30.
   C:      OK, check in any time after 3:00 P.M. and your room will be ready.
   Ms. G:  Oh, could you make sure it is a non-smoking room, please? I just can't stand the smell of cigarette smoke.
   C:      Yes, certainly.

   Ms. G:  And could you make sure it is a quiet room? I don't want to be overlooking the parking lot or anything like that.
   C:      Yes, of course.
   Ms. G:  Does the room price include breakfast?
   C:      Yes, it does. Breakfast is served in our restaurant from 7:00 A.M.
   Ms. G:  That's good. I'd like to be not too far away from the restaurant, please. Do all the rooms have cable TV?
   C:      Yes, they do.
   Ms. G:  And room service?
   C:      Yes, you'll find a flyer containing all the information about our hotel services in your room. If you have any questions, just call the front desk.
   Ms. G:  OK. Thank you. Oh, just one more thing.
   C:      Yes?
   Ms. G:  How much does it cost?

3. Ask volunteers for the answers.

**Answers:**
price, type of room, location of room, meals, cable TV

## Part 2

1. Have students read the directions and look at the form.

2. Play or read the conversation again and tell students to listen for the details to fill in the chart.

3. Play or read the conversation again for students to check their answers.

4. Ask volunteers for the answers.

> **Answers:**
> Ms. Emily Gardiner; June 28th to June 30th; a single, non-smoking, quiet room

## Part 3

1. Have students read the directions.

2. Pair Work. Have students take turns asking and answering questions about what is available at the Palm Tree Hotel.

3. Ask some pairs to demonstrate for the class.

**Student Book page 65**

## Let's Talk

## Part 1

1. Have students read the directions and look at the questions.

2. Give students time to think of how to describe their dream hotel.

3. Group Work. Have students ask each other the questions and discuss their dream hotel. Make sure they write their answers.

## Part 2

1. Have students read the directions and look at the chart.

2. Give students time to think of questions to ask the other students about their hotels.

3. Class Work. Have students walk around the class and interview other students about their hotel. If they like the hotel, tell them to make a reservation.

4. Circulate and help as needed.

## Part 3

1. Have students read the directions for the activity.

2. Group Work. Have students return to their original groups. Have students report how many reservations they got and which hotels they made a reservation for.

3. Have each group report their discussion to the class. Have a class vote on which hotel seemed the most interesting. Have students explain their votes.

# We'd like to check in, please.

Student Book page 66

Review. Pretend to be a tourist and "call" one of the "travel agents" in the class. Ask two or three questions about a hotel. Have the "travel agent" now pretend to be a customer and call another student in the class. Continue quickly around the classroom.

## Vocabulary

Introduce these words and phrases to the students:

*check in:* register at a hotel

*with an ocean view:* with windows from where one can see the ocean

*(diving) gear:* the equipment needed for diving

*We can manage.:* We can do it without help.

## Prelistening

1. Have students open their books and look at the photograph. Ask:

   - *Where are the speakers?* (at the front desk of a hotel)
   - *Where is the hotel located?* (near the beach, in Tioman)

2. Pair Work. Read the title of the conversation and the prelistening questions. Have the pairs take turns asking and answering the questions.

3. Have pairs share their answers with the class.

## Conversation 2

Class CD 2, Track 17

1. With books closed, play the recording or read the conversation.

   Julie:  We'd like to check in, please.
   Clerk:  Do you have a reservation?
   Julie:  Yes, our last names are Park and Kim.
   Clerk:  Here it is. Could you sign here, please? And I'll need to see your passports.
   Julie:  Here you are. Do you have a room with an ocean view?
   Clerk:  Yes, we do. You can have room 43B.
   Lisa:   And do you know where we can rent some diving gear?
   Clerk:  You can rent diving equipment from our diving center, just around the corner from the swimming pool. It's open from 7 A.M. to 3 P.M.
   Julie:  And what time can we get dinner?
   Clerk:  The restaurant opens for dinner from 6:00 P.M.
   Julie:  Thanks.
   Clerk:  Do you need any help with your bags?

   Lisa:   No, that's all right. We can manage.

2. Ask these comprehension questions:

   - *What are the women doing?* (checking in)
   - *Do they have a reservation?* (yes)

3. Say: *Listen again. This time listen for the information given by the clerk.*

4. Play or read the conversation again, pausing for choral repetition. Allow students to write down the information as they listen. Play or read the conversation again, if needed, for students to get all the information.

5. Ask the following questions:

   - *What does the clerk ask to see?* (the women's passports)
   - *What kind of room do the women ask for?* (one with an ocean view)
   - *What do they want to rent?* (diving gear)
   - *Where can they rent it?* (in the diving center around the corner from the swimming pool)
   - *What time is the diving center open?* (from 7 A.M. to 3 P.M.)
   - *What time does the restaurant open for dinner?* (6 P.M.)

   Elicit responses from various students.

## PRONUNCIATION FOCUS

Class CD 2, Track 18

1. Explain what the focus is. Play or read the examples in the book and have students repeat chorally.

   **Do you know where we can rent some diving gear?**
   **What time can we get dinner?**
   **We can manage.**

2. With books open, play or read the conversation again. Tell students to pay attention to the unstressed examples of *can.*

3. Paired Reading. Have students practice the conversation, switching roles.

## Give It a Try

## 1. Checking in

### Presentation

1. Have students look at the function box. Give them time to read the examples.

2. Model the exchanges and have students repeat chorally.

### Note

Point out that the sentence *The name is (Park).* is used in confirming reservations and other official business.

### Practice

**Class CD 2, Track 19**

1. Have students read the directions.

2. Play or read the example conversation.

> A: I'd like to check in, please.
> B: Do you have a reservation?
> A: Yes, the last name is Park.
> B: Here it is. Could you sign here, please?

3. Pair Work. Have students take turns being a hotel guest and a desk clerk.

4. Have pairs demonstrate their exchanges for the class.

## 2. Making requests

### Notes

1. Many hotels have both smoking and non-smoking rooms. It is often necessary for the guest to request his or her preference.

2. A room that is *taken* is already occupied. In many public places, such as a movie theater, a park, or a baseball stadium, *Is this seat taken?* can be used to inquire if a particular seat is available.

3. Explain that in rapid speech *could I have* and *do you have* are often reduced and blended. The stress is put on the content words. On the board, write the following sentences without marking the content words:

*Could I have a <u>room</u> with an <u>ocean view</u>?*

*Do you have a <u>non-smoking</u> <u>room</u>?*

*Could I have a <u>room</u> <u>near the pool</u>?*

Have volunteers mark the content words in each question and pronounce the question. Model each question and have students repeat.

### Presentation

1. Have students look at the function box. Give them time to read the examples.

2. Model the exchanges and have students repeat chorally.

### Practice

**Class CD 2, Track 20**

1. Have students read the directions and look at the words in the box, the list, and the floor plan.

2. Play or read the example conversation.

> A: Do you have a room with an ocean view?
> B: Yes, certainly. You can have room 43B.

3. Pair Work. Have students take turns making and answering requests.

4. Have pairs demonstrate their exchanges for the class.

## 3. Asking about hotel services

### Presentation

1. Have students look at the function box. Give them time to read the examples.

2. Model the exchanges in the function box and have students repeat chorally.

3. Practice a few exchanges with various students.

### Practice

**Class CD 2, Track 21**

1. Have students read the directions and look at the hotel information and the questions. Go over anything students don't understand.

2. Do a quick scanning exercise with students. Ask questions such as: *Do they serve dinner? Are there wake-up calls?*

3. Play or read the example conversation twice.

> A: Can I help you?
> B: Could you tell me what time the restaurant opens for breakfast?
> A: Yes, of course. Breakfast is served in the restaurant from 7:30 A.M. to 10:00 A.M.
> B: Thank you very much.

4. Pair Work. Have students take turns being the clerk and the guest.

5. Have pairs demonstrate their conversation for the class.

## Listen to This

Class CD 2, Track 22

### Part 1

1. Give students time to read the directions and look at the chart.

2. Play or read the conversations. Tell students to write each guest's request in the chart.

**1**

Mr. M: I'd like to check in, please.

C: Certainly. Do you have a reservation?

Mr. M: Yes. The name is Morales. Mr. and Mrs. J. Morales.

C: Here we are. For five nights. Could you fill out the registration card, please? And I'll need your credit card.

Mr. M: All right.

C: Thank you. And here's your room key. Room 826.

Mr. M: Does that room have an ocean view?

C: No. Rooms with an ocean view are $15.00 more per night. Your room overlooks...the parking lot.

Mr. M: Well, we'd like a room with an ocean view, please.

C: I'm sorry. Those rooms are all taken.

**2**

C: Front desk. Can I help you?

Mr. B: This is Mr. Burton in 1205. Can I get a wake-up call, please?

C: Of course. What time?

Mr. B: Five o'clock.

C: That's no problem. We'll be happy to do that. Anything else?

Mr. B: No. That's it. Thank you.

**3**

G: (To herself) I really overslept. Oh, boy. Eleven o'clock. I need something to eat. I'm starving.

C: Front desk. Can I help you?

G: Yeah, hi. This is Gale Martin in room 327. Is breakfast still being served?

C: I'm sorry. Breakfast finishes at 10:30 A.M.

G: Oh, no. Well, do you know where I can get some breakfast?

C: Just call Room Service at extension 121. You can order some food from them. They'll send it up to your room.

G: OK, thanks. I'll give them a call.

3. Check answers.

> **Answers:**
> 1. an ocean view
> 2. a wake-up call
> 3. room service

### Part 2

1. Give students time to read the directions.

2. Tell students to listen again and write the name and room number of each guest.

3. Play or read the conversations.

4. Check answers.

> **Answers:**
> 1. Mr. and Mrs. J. Morales; 826
> 2. Mr. Burton; 1205
> 3. Gale Martin; 327

### Part 3

1. Give students time to read the directions.

2. Tell students to listen if the requests were successful or not.

3. Play or read the conversation.

4. Check answers.

> **Answers:** 1. no   2. yes   3. yes

## Person to Person

**Part 1**

1. Divide the class into pairs and have students decide who will be Student A and who will be Student B. Remind Students B to look at page 111.

2. Have students read the directions and look at the brochure.

3. Give Students A time to think of what questions they need to ask to fill in the information on their brochure. Exemplify the first question, if necessary: *How many Deluxe suites are there in the hotel?*

4. Pair Work. Have Student A ask Student B questions and fill in the missing information.

5. Circulate and help as needed.

**Part 2**

1. Have students read the directions.

2. Give Students B time to think of what questions they need to ask to fill in the information on their brochure.

3. Pair Work. Have Student B ask Student A questions and fill in the missing information.

4. Circulate and help as needed.

**Part 3**

1. Have students read the directions.

2. Give Students A time to think of what questions they need to ask to make their reservation.

3. Pair Work. Have Student A role-play calling Student B and making a reservation. Circulate and help as needed.

4. Have several pairs demonstrate their conversations for the class.

## Now Try This

1. Have students read the directions.

2. Give students time to think of their ideal hotel and to think of questions to ask their partner about their dream hotel.

3. Pair Work. Have students take turns asking and answering questions about each other's dream hotel. Tell students to take notes.

4. Have several students report their partner's answers to the class.

## Components

Student Book, pages 70–77, 112
Class CD 2, Tracks 23–31
Optional Activities 9.1–9.2,
page 110

## Objectives

**Functions:** Getting information,
discussing possible activities, asking
about public transportation, talking
about tours

**Topics:** Travel, sight-seeing itineraries,
tourist activities, using public
transportation, guided tours

**Structures:** Review of *should* and *can*,
conditionals

**Pronunciation Focus:** Linking of
final [t] sound to initial vowel sound
of next word

**Listen to This:** Listening for specific
information: descriptions of places,
details of a tour; filling in a chart,
answering questions

---

**Student Book page 70**

## CONSIDER THIS

1. Have students read the text and the question. Go over any vocabulary students don't know.

2. Group Work. Divide students into groups of four or five. Have students in each group discuss what they think is the world's (or their country's) best cities to visit. Help students with vocabulary as needed.

3. Ask volunteers for their answers.

### Vocabulary

Introduce these words and phrases to the students:

*sights:* places of interest visited by tourists

*cable car:* vehicle supported by cables, usually for taking tourists up a mountain

*lots:* many

*street market:* an outdoor market

*You name it.:* anything you can imagine

### Prelistening

1. Pair Work. Have students open their books and look at the photograph. Have partners describe what they see to each other. Circulate and help with vocabulary as needed.

2. Class Work. Read the title of the conversation and the prelistening question. Ask volunteers to answer the question.

## Conversation 1

**Class CD 2, Track 23**

1. With books closed, play the recording or read the conversation.

   Sang-woo: Hi. Can you help me? I'm here for a week and I need some ideas for things to do.

   Guide 1:　I have some brochures here. What are you interested in seeing here in Hong Kong?

   Sang-woo: First, I want to see the famous sights.

   Guide 1:　Of course, you shouldn't miss Victoria Peak. You take a cable car to the top, and you can get fantastic views of the city from there.

   Sang-woo: That's a good idea. What else is there to do?

   Guide 1:　Hundreds of things! If you like shopping, there are lots of street markets where you can get really good bargains on clothing, antiques...whatever you like.

   Sang-woo: I'm not really interested in that. What's there to do at night?

   Guide 1:　There are clubs, concerts, plays...you name it.

   Sang-woo: That sounds exciting!

2. Ask these comprehension questions:

   • *Where are the speakers?* (at an information desk)
   • *What city are they in?* (Hong Kong)

3. Play or read the conversation again, pausing for choral repetition.

---

4. Ask the following questions:

- *How long will Speaker 1 be in Hong Kong?* (one week)
- *What does he want to see?* (famous sights)
- *What other things does Speaker 2 suggest?* (Victoria Peak, street markets, clubs, concerts, plays)
- *What isn't Speaker 1 interested in?* (street markets)

Elicit responses from various students.

5. Paired Reading. Have students read the conversation, switching roles.

Student Book page 71

## Give It a Try

## 1. Getting Information

### Presentation

1. Have students look at the function box. Give them time to read the examples.

2. Model the exchanges and have students repeat chorally.

3. Practice a few exchanges with various students.

### Note

Explain that in rapid speech, *what do you* often sounds like /wuh-duh-ya/. On the board, write the following:

<u>What do you</u> want to see?

<u>What do you</u> want to do?

Model and have students repeat.

### Practice 1

Class CD 2, Track 24

1. Have students read the directions and look at the list and the picture of Victoria Peak in Hong Kong. Go over vocabulary, if necessary.

2. Play or read the example conversation twice.

   A: I need some ideas for things to do in Hong Kong.
   B: What are you interested in seeing?
   A: First, I want to see the famous sights.
   B: You shouldn't miss Victoria Peak. You can get fantastic views from there. Then you can go shopping.

3. Pair Work. Have students decide who will be Student A and who will be Student B. Have Student B ask Student A questions about what to do in Hong Kong.

4. Ask several pairs to demonstrate for the class.

### Practice 2

1. Have students read the directions and look at the list and the picture of Old Chinatown in Singapore. Go over vocabulary, if necessary.

2. Play or read the example conversation again, twice.

3. Pair Work. Have Student A ask Student B questions about what to do in Singapore.

4. Ask several pairs to demonstrate for the class.

### Extension

1. Have students think of three or four things to do and see in their city or town. Divide students into pairs. Have them role-play a tourist and a guide and take turns asking and answering about what to do in their town or city. Make sure the "guides" suggest different things to do and see.

2. Do the above activity, but this time have students think of another country, city, or town that they have visited or know about, and think of things to do and see there. Have several pairs demonstrate for the class.

## 2. Discussing possible activities

### Presentation

1.  Have students look at the function box. Give them time to read the examples.

2.  Model the exchanges and have students repeat chorally.

3.  Have various pairs practice the exchanges with different combinations.

### Note

Explain that *you* is often used in English to mean *any person* or *somebody*.

### Practice 1

**Class CD 2, Track 25**

1.  Have students read the directions and look at the list and the words in the box. Go over vocabulary, if necessary.

2.  Review the pictures and information on the previous page.

3.  Play or read the example conversation twice.

    A: What is there to do?
    B: If you like shopping, there are lots of street markets.
    A: I'm not really interested in that. What else is there to do?

4.  Pair Work. Have students take turns asking each other about activities in Hong Kong or Singapore.

5.  Ask several pairs to demonstrate for the class.

### Practice 2

1.  Have students read the directions and look at the pictures. Give students time to think of things to do in each location. Brainstorm some ideas for each place, if necessary.

2.  Pair Work. Have students take turns asking and answering questions about what to do in each of the locations.

3.  Ask several pairs to demonstrate for the class.

### Extension

1.  Class Discussion. Discuss with students the kinds of things they like to do on a vacation.

2.  Have students use their dictionaries to add words to the **Use These Words** list.

## Listen to This

**Class CD 2, Track 26**

### Part 1

1.  Have students read the directions and look at the chart.

2.  Play or read the descriptions. Tell students to listen for the name of each place and write it on the chart.

    **1**

    Vietnam is the ideal holiday destination for travelers who like the unusual and the unique. Go sight-seeing in Hanoi, the 1,000-year-old capital city of Vietnam, a unique blend of eastern and western charm with brightly painted temples and pagodas side by side with elegant French colonial buildings.

    Visit the Temple of Literature, the site of Vietnam's first university, which dates back to 1070, the One Pillar Pagoda, first built in 1049, which resembles a lotus blossom rising out of the water, and Ho Chi Minh's Mausoleum, the burial place of the famous leader who led Vietnam to independence.

    Enjoy Hanoi's cuisine and linger over a cup of coffee in one of its sidewalk cafes. Spend an evening at the traditional water puppet theater. Originally performed on lakes and ponds, these productions take place in a theater with a stage knee-deep in water.

    If you like shopping, you won't be bored! Browse the 36 streets of the Old Quarter where each street was originally named after the product sold there, for example, Fish Street, Tin Street, and Bamboo Street. Bargains include silk, embroidery, handicrafts, and original works of art.

    **2**

    Guam is a tropical paradise! The island's dramatic coastline and white sand beaches are ringed by coral reefs and crystal clear waters full of exotic marine life.

    Visit the underwater observatories and discover 300 types of coral. Go diving for buried treasure among the shipwrecks. Take a boat tour to go dolphin-watching.

    If you like water sports, the island of Guam is the place for you! There are ocean sports for the whole family, including banana boat rides, kayaking, pedal boats, parasailing, snorkeling, windsurfing, and wake boarding.

3.  Ask volunteers for the answers.

    **Answers:** 1. Vietnam     2. Guam

## Part 2

1. Have students read the directions.

2. Play or read the conversation again and tell students to listen for what they can see and do in each place and write them in the chart.

3. Play or read the conversation again for students to check their answers.

4. Ask volunteers for the answers.

> **Possible Answers:**
> 1. Hanoi, temples, pagodas, French colonial buildings, The Temple of Literature, the One Pillar Pagoda, Ho Chi Minh's Mausoleum, cafes, water puppet theater, shopping, Old Quarter
> 2. beaches, underwater observatories, diving, dolphin-watching, ocean sports (banana boat rides, kayaking, pedal boats, parasailing, snorkeling, windsurfing, wake boarding)

## Part 3

1. Have students read the directions.

2. Group Work. Have students discuss which of the two vacations is better for families. Have them discuss if their answers are different for a family with young children than for a family with teenagers.

3. Have each group report their discussion to the class.

**Student Book page 73**

## Let's Talk

### Part 1

1. Have students read the directions and look at the chart.

2. Give students time to think of three things they like to do on vacation. Brainstorm ideas as a class, if necessary.

3. Have students write their three things in the chart.

### Part 2

1. Have students read the directions.

2. Class Work. Have students walk around the class and take turns asking each other for advice about where to go on vacation. Tell them to write the places that match their favorite activities in their charts. Make sure that if they don't know what kinds of things they can do in a place that another student suggests, they ask that student questions about what they can do there.

3. Circulate and help as needed.

### Part 3

1. Have students read the directions.

2. Have various students tell the class which places they wrote down and which place they would choose and why.

### Part 4

1. Have students read the directions.

2. Pair Work. Have students discuss their top five most important things when choosing a vacation destination.

3. Class Work. Have each pair report their lists to the class. List the students' answers on the board and have the class vote on the top five most important things. Discuss with the class why their choices are important to them.

### *Extension*

Write the names of famous places on slips of paper. Have a student choose a paper and say what kind of vacation a single person, a couple, or a family could have there.

# How do I get there?

**Student Book page 74**

Review. Ask several students where they like to go on vacation and what kinds of things they like to do there.

## *Vocabulary*

Introduce these words and phrases to the students:

*catch:* get, take

*points of interest:* places that many people want to visit

*per person:* for each person

## *Prelistening*

1. Have students open their books and look at the photograph. Ask:

   - *Where are the speakers?* (at a tourist information booth)
   - *What do you think the tourist is asking for?* (directions)

2. Pair Work. Read the title of the conversation and the prelistening question. Have students discuss the question in pairs.

3. Class Work. Have pairs share their answers with the class. Have the class choose the best ideas.

## Conversation 2

**Class CD 2, Track 27**

1. With books closed, play the recording or read the conversation.

   Sang-woo: What's the best way to get to Waterfront Park from here? Can I take the subway?

   Guide: No, but you can catch the number 34 bus in front of that hotel. Get off at Harbor Street. Actually, it's just a short walk from here.

   Sang-woo: Really? How far is it?

   Guide: About ten or fifteen minutes. You know, there are also guided tours of the city you can take.

   Sang-woo: Oh? What does the city tour include?

   Guide: They take you around the major points of interest. You can get a good idea of where everything is.

   Sang-woo: Hmm. How much is it?

   Guide: It's $10.00 per person for a one-hour tour. The tour bus stops across the street from here, and there should be one in about ten minutes. You can buy a ticket on the bus.

   Sang-woo: Thanks. That sounds like a great idea.

2. Ask these comprehension questions:

   - *Where does Speaker 1 want to go?* (to the Waterfront Park)
   - *How can he get there?* (by bus)
   - *How far is it?* (ten or fifteen minutes)

3. Say: *Listen again. This time listen for the information about the guided tours.*

4. Play or read the conversation again, pausing for choral repetition. Allow students to write down the information as they listen. Play or read the conversation again, if needed, for students to get all the information.

5. Ask the following questions:

   - *What does the city tour include?* (all the major points of interest)
   - *How much is it?* ($10.00 per person)
   - *How long is the tour?* (one hour)
   - *When will the next tour bus come?* (in about ten minutes)
   - *Where can you buy a ticket?* (on the bus)

Elicit responses from various students.

## PRONUNCIATION FOCUS

**Class CD 2, Track 28**

1. Explain what the focus is. Play or read the examples in the book and have students repeat chorally.

   | front of | get off |
   |----------|---------|
   | just a   | get a   |

2. With books open, play or read the conversation again. Tell students to pay attention to the linked words.

3. Paired Reading. Have students practice the conversation, switching roles.

## Give It a Try

# 1. Asking about public transportation

## Presentation

1. Have students look at the function box. Give them time to read the examples.

2. Model the exchanges and have students repeat chorally.

3. Practice a few exchanges with different combinations with various students.

### Note

Remind students that heavier stress is placed on the content words in sentences that give directions. On the board, write the following sentences without marking the stressed words:

*How do I get to Waterfront Park?*

*Can I take a bus?*

*You can catch the number 34 bus.*

*You can take the subway to the Museum Station.*

Have volunteers come to the board and mark the content words. Then have them read the sentences aloud. Model each sentence and have students repeat.

## Practice 1

**Class CD 2, Track 29**

1. Have students read the directions and look at the list and the schedule.

2. To check comprehension, ask:

   *Can I take a subway to Harper's Bay Mall?* (no)

   *What is the best way to get to the Opera House?* (take the subway to King Station)

3. Play or read the example conversation twice.

   A: Excuse me. What's the best way to get to Waterfront Park from here? Can I take a bus?
   B: Yes, you can catch the number 34 bus.

4. Pair Work. Have students take turns asking and answering questions about how to get to the places on the list.

5. Ask several pairs to demonstrate for the class.

## Practice 2

1. Have students read the directions and look at the subway map and the stations in Practice 1.

2. To check comprehension, ask:

   *How do I get to Baker Station?* (take the Red line to Main Station and then change to the Yellow line to Baker Station)

3. Pair Work. Have students take turns asking and answering questions about how to get to the subway stations from Practice 1.

4. Ask several pairs to demonstrate for the class.

## Extension

Bring in maps of famous cities from guide books or websites. Have groups plan a three-day trip in that city and organize how to get to each point of interest they choose using public transportation. Have each group report on their trips.

## 2. Talking about tours

### Presentation

1. Have students look at the function box. Give them time to read the examples.

2. Model the exchanges and have students repeat chorally.

3. Practice a few exchanges with various students.

### Note

Explain to the students that in an expression where a number+noun precedes a noun, the noun that follows the number is usually singular. For example: *a two-hour tour*, *several three-meter lines*, etc.

### Practice 1

**Class CD 2, Track 30**

1. Divide the class into pairs. Have students decide who will be Student A and who will be Student B.

2. Have students read the directions and look at their respective posters and the word box.

3. Play or read the example conversation twice.

   A: What does the city tour include?
   B: They take you around the major points of interest.

4. Pair Work. Have Student A cover the poster of the walking tour and ask Student B questions about the tour.

5. Ask several pairs to demonstrate for the class.

### Practice 2

1. Have students read the directions and look at the words in the box.

2. Pair Work. Have Student B cover the harbor tour poster and ask Student A questions about the tour.

3. Ask several pairs to demonstrate for the class.

### Extension

Have students use their dictionaries to add words to the **Use These Words** list.

## Listen to This

**Class CD 2, Track 31**

### Part 1

1. Have students read the directions for the activity.

2. Play or read the tour guide's talk. Tell students to listen for what kind of tour it is.

G:    Welcome aboard our trolleybus tour of downtown Minneapolis. We are delighted to have you aboard.

I'll be collecting your tickets in a moment. If you don't have your ticket yet, please go to the ticket stand on the corner, and they'll be happy to help you. Tickets are $20.00 each.

The tour lasts two hours. Our tour today includes all the highlights of our beautiful downtown and also the historic St. Anthony's Falls heritage zone. There will be a 30-minute break for lunch at the Nicollet Mall. That's a great place to stroll around, and the food court has a wide variety of meals and snacks. At the end of the tour, we'll drop you off right here where we picked you up, outside the Walker Art Center.

OK. My name is Annalisa and I'm going to be your guide today. I was born and brought up right here in Minneapolis, and I reckon I know the city pretty well. But you may well come up with a question I can't answer. That happens sometimes! Please ask questions. That makes the ride so much more interesting! And please tell me if you want to stop to take pictures. I'm happy to do that. Now, where are you all from?

P:    Florida! Japan! England!

3. Ask volunteers for the answer.

**Answer:**
a trolleybus tour of the highlights of downtown and the heritage zone

### Part 2

1. Have students read the directions for and look at the questions.

2. Play or read the talk again and tell students to listen for the answers to the questions.

3. Play or read the talk again for students to check their answers.

4. Ask volunteers for the answers.

**Answers:**
1. $20.00 per person
2. two hours
3. thirty minutes
4. outside the Walker Art Center

**Part 3**

1. Have students read the directions for the activity.

2. Play or read the talk again for students to check their answers.

3. Give students time to think of questions about the information given in the talk.

4. Pair Work. Have students take turns asking each other three more questions about the tour guide's introduction.

5. Have pairs ask their questions to the rest of the class.

## Extension

Have groups write an introduction to a tour of their town or city. Have one person in the group read the introduction to the class. Have the class ask questions about the things they will see on the tour.

**Student Book pages 77 & 112**

## Person to Person

**Part 1**

1. Divide the class into pairs and have students decide who will be Student A and who will be Student B. Remind Students B to look at page 112.

2. Have students read the directions and look at the map. Ask if any students have been to or know anything about Vancouver.

3. Give students time to think of either places to recommend seeing (Student A) or places to get more information about (Student B).

4. To check comprehension, ask:

   *Student A, what is one place you would recommend seeing? Why do you recommend it?*

   *Student B, what is one place you want more information about? What do you want to know about it?*

   Brainstorm possible questions and answers, if necessary.

4. Have students write down their recommendations and questions. Circulate and help as needed.

**Part 2**

1. Have students read the directions.

2. Pair Work. Have students role-play being a tour guide and a visitor to Vancouver.

3. Circulate and help as needed.

4. Have several pairs demonstrate part of their role-play for the class.

**Part 3**

1. Have students read the directions.

2. Give students time to think of what sights he or she should definitely visit.

3. Pair Work. Have students discuss which places definitely should be visited. Make sure students give specific reasons for their choices.

4. Have pairs report their discussions to the class. Discuss as a class which sight is the number one place to visit in Vancouver.

## Extension

1. Class Discussion. Have the class discuss places they have been to and say which places of interest should definitely be visited there.

2. Class Discussion. Have students discuss which cities or places in the world should be visited by everyone.

## Note

In each discussion above, make sure students give specific reasons for their choices.

## Now Try This

1. Have students read the directions.

2. Give students time to think of a place they have been to and what to see there.

3. Pair Work. Have students take turns talking about what to see in a place they have visited.

4. Have several students report their partner's recommendations to the class.

# Review:
## Units 7–9

**Components**

Student Book, pages 78–79
Class CD 2, tracks 32–34

**Student Book page 78**

## Listen To This Unit 7

**Class CD 2, Track 32**

1. Have students read the directions and look at the chart.

2. Play or read the instructions. Ask students to listen for the tools first.

   First, let's talk about the things you'll need. You'll need some liquid glue, some newspaper torn into long strips, a balloon, some plastic food wrap, and a pin. OK? Got that?
   Now let's talk about the instructions. The first thing you have to do is blow up the balloon. Next, cover the balloon with plastic food wrap. After that, cover the food wrap with glue. This gets really messy! OK, next take the strips of newspaper, and put them over the glued area. They should go around the balloon. Then cover it with glue again. You'll probably want to put 15 to 20 layers of newspaper on. After that, let it dry thoroughly. It might take a day or two. Finally, put a pin through it and pop the balloon, and there you have it!

3. Have students fill in the first column in the chart.

4. Play or read the instructions again. Ask students to note down the steps this time.

5. If necessary, play or read the instructions again for students to check their answers.

6. Ask volunteers for their answers.

> **Answers:**
> Tools: liquid glue, newspaper torn into strips, a balloon, plastic food wrap, a pin
> Steps:
> 1. blow up the balloon
> 2. cover the balloon with plastic food wrap
> 3. cover the food wrap with glue
> 4. put the newspaper strips over the glue
> 5. cover the strips with glue (cover the balloon with 15 or 16 layers of newspaper)
> 6. let dry and pop the balloon It's a papier-mache ball.

## Give It a Try

1. Have students read the directions and look at the list of items. Go over vocabulary, if necessary.

2. Group Work. Have students discuss which five items to take with them.

3. Class Work. Have groups compare their lists. Have a class discussion to choose the five most important items.

## Listen To This Unit 8

**Class CD 2, Track 33**

1. Have students read the directions and look at the question and the list of facilities and services.

2. Play or read the conversation.

   C: Hi. Can I help you?
   W: Yes, I'd like a room for the night, please. The sign outside says you have vacancies.
   C: Yes, but only a couple.
   W: How much are the rooms?
   C: They're $50.00 a night.
   W: That's fine.
   C: I can give you room 14. I just need you to sign the register.
   W: There you go. I'm awfully hungry. Is the restaurant still open?
   C: We don't have a restaurant, but the coffee shop is open until nine o'clock. If you want anything after that, there are a couple of vending machines for soft drinks, chocolate bars—things like that.
   W: Thank you. By the way, is there a television in the room?
   C: Yes, there is, we've got cable TV.
   W: Oh, that's great.
   C: Well, here's your room key. If you need anything else, more towels or anything, the office is open until midnight.
   W: I wonder if I could get a wake-up call for 6:00 A.M. tomorrow?
   C: Well, you'll find an alarm clock in your room. I am afraid that's the best we can do.
   W: OK. Thanks again.

3. Have students answer the question and check the facilities and services available.

4. Ask volunteers for the answers.

**Answers:**
1. $50.00 a night
2. coffee shop, vending machines, cable TV

**Student Book page 79**

## Give It a Try

1. Have students read the directions and look at the charts.

2. Pair Work. Give students time to fill in the chart for their dream hotel. Have students take turns asking each other about their dream hotels and filling in the other chart. Then have each student make a reservation.

3. Have several pairs role-play for the class, asking for information about one of their hotels and making a reservation.

## Listen To This Unit 9

**Class CD 2, Track 34**

1. Have students read the directions and look at the chart and the picture of the double-decker bus. Teach students the word *double-decker*.

2. Play or read the description of the tour.

Enjoy the best of London's sights—from the top of an open-topped double-decker bus. Our full-day tour of London includes all the famous highlights and legendary landmarks of this historic city, such as the Tower of London, Big Ben, and Westminster Abbey. Relax and enjoy the fantastic views while listening to an entertaining and informative commentary from one of our expert guides. Recorded commentaries in languages other than English are available on request. Complimentary soft drinks are available.

Tickets are $35.00 for adults and $15.00 for children under 14. The tour lasts approximately two hours. Tickets can be purchased from the Information Center, selected hotels or, easiest of all, on the buses themselves. Keep your ticket and get on and off the tour bus to explore points of interest along the way. Or stop for lunch, which is not included in the tour, in one of London's many historic pubs. You can board any of our tour routes at over 90 different stops around the city. Buses run every 10 to 20 minutes.

The ticket price also includes a river cruise between Westminster Abbey and the Tower of London.

Hop on board for an unforgettable experience.

3. Have students fill in the chart.

4. Ask volunteers for the answers.

**Answers:**

| See: | all famous highlights and legendary landmarks |
|---|---|
| Cost/Time: | $35.00 for adults; $15.00 for children under 14; two hours |
| Included: | commentary from guide, recorded commentaries in other languages, soft drinks, river cruise |
| Not included: | lunch |

## Give It a Try

**Part 1**

1. Have students read the directions and look at the chart.

2. Group Work. Give students time to plan a tour of their town or neighborhood and write down four places to visit. Have groups discuss the reasons to visit each place.

**Part 2**

1. Have students read the directions.

2. Pair Work. Have each student get together with someone from another group. Have them take turns role-playing being a tourist and a tour guide using the information from their charts.

## Components

Student Book, pages 80–87, 113
Class CD 2, Tracks 35–43
Optional Activities 10.1–10.2,
pages 110–111

## Objectives

**Functions:** Asking who someone is, identifying someone, asking what someone is like, discussing qualities

**Topics:** Personal descriptions, positive and negative characteristics

**Structures:** Relative clauses, adjectives for personal description, modifiers

**Pronunciation Focus:** [r] sound after a vowel

**Listen to This:** Listening for specific information: names, detailed information, descriptions; filling in charts

---

**Student Book page 80**

## CONSIDER THIS

1. Have students read the text and the question. Go over vocabulary students don't know.

2. Group Work. Divide students into groups of four or five. Have students in each group read and then take turns asking and answering the question. Help students with vocabulary as needed.

3. Ask the groups to report the qualities the students in the group look for in a partner. Make a master list on the board. Compare the class results with the U.S. survey results.

### *Prelistening*

1. Pair Work. Have students open their books and look at the photograph. Have partners describe what they see to each other. Circulate and help with vocabulary as needed.

2. Class Work. Read the title of the conversation and the prelistening task and question. Have volunteers describe the people in the picture. Write the adjectives they use on the board.

## Conversation 1

**Class CD 2, Track 35**

1. With books closed, play the recording or read the conversation.

   Mariko: I've been here nearly six months, and I still don't know half the people here. Who's that woman?

   Bob: Where?

   Mariko: The one in the purple sweater.

   Bon: I don't know. I never saw her before. Why?

   Mariko: I think she's the one who just moved into my apartment building.

   Bob: Oh, yeah?

   Mariko: And do you know who that man is?

   Bob: Which one?

   Mariko: The one in the blue jacket. I think I've met him before.

   Bob: That's Matt Chang.

   Mariko: Is he the one whose brother drives the red sports car?

   Bob: Yeah, that's right.

   Mariko: Well, Matt's the one I'd like to meet. Can you introduce me to him?

2. Ask these comprehension questions:

   • *Where are the speakers?* (in a hallway in a college)
   • *How long has Speaker 1 been there?* (six months)
   • *Does Speaker 1 know lots of people there?* (no)

3. Play or read the conversation again, pausing for choral repetition.

4. Ask the following questions:
   - *Does Speaker 2 know the woman in the purple sweater?* (no)
   - *Who does Speaker 1 think she is?* (someone who just moved into her apartment building)
   - *Does Speaker 2 know the man in the blue jacket?* (yes)
   - *Who is he?* (Matt Chang)
   - *What does Matt Chang's brother drive?* (a red sports car)
   - *Who does Speaker 1 want to meet?* (Matt Chang's brother)

   Elicit responses from various students.

5. Paired Reading. Have students read the conversation, switching roles.

**Student Book page 81**

## Give It a Try

## 1. Asking who someone is

### Presentation

1. Have students look at the function box. Give them time to read the examples.

2. Model the exchanges and have students repeat chorally.

3. Practice a few exchanges with various students.

### Notes

1. Explain the use of *who* replacing the subject (when a person) in relative clauses. For example:

   *That's the guy. He just moved in.*

   *That's the guy who just moved in.*

2. Explain that *I have no idea* is used when the speaker wants to emphasize that he or she does not know something. *I never saw him before in my life* is also used in casual conversation to emphasize that the speaker does not know someone.

3. Explain that when using a physical description to refer to another person, you must be careful not to refer to sensitive traits. Hair color, eye color, and height are all safe, but weight, age, or specific descriptions of other physical features can be too sensitive and should be avoided.

### Practice 1

Class CD 2, Track 36

1. Have students read the directions and look at the pictures and the list. Go over vocabulary, if necessary.

2. To check comprehension, ask students to describe the people in each picture.

3. Play or read the example conversation twice.

   A: Who's that woman?
   B: Which one?
   A: The one in the purple sweater.
   B: She's the one who just moved into my apartment building.

4. Pair Work. Have students take turns asking and answering questions about the people in each picture.

5. Ask several pairs to demonstrate for the class.

### Practice 2

1. Have students read the directions.

2. To check comprehension, have students practice describing other students in the class in several ways, for example: the woman with the red handbag; the man in the second row; the woman with the dark hair and blue eyes.

3. Pair Work. Have students take turns asking and answering questions about the other students in the class.

4. Ask several pairs to demonstrate for the class.

## 2. Identifying someone

Review. Have a student describe another student in the class without saying who the person is. Have the other students guess who is being described. Repeat with several students, asking them to describe the other students in different ways.

### Presentation

1. Have students look at the function boxes. Give them time to read the examples.

2. Model the exchanges and have students repeat chorally.

3. Practice a few exchanges with various students.

### Notes

1. Explain the use of *whose* replacing the possessive adjective in relative clauses. For example:

   *She's the one. Her husband just got a new job.*

   *She's the one whose husband just got a new job.*

2. Remind students that Yes/No questions have rising intonation. On the board, write the following questions and mark the intonation:

   *Is he the one whose brother drives a red sports car?*

   *Isn't she the one whose father is a doctor?*

Model the questions and have students repeat.

### Practice 1

**Class CD 2, Track 37**

1. Have students read the directions and look at the pictures and the captions. Go over vocabulary, if necessary.

2. To check comprehension, have several students describe one of the people in the pictures.

3. Play or read the example conversation twice.

   A: Is Matt the one whose brother drives the red sports car?
   B: Yes, that's right.

4. Pair Work. Have students decide who will be Student A and who will be Student B. Have students take turns asking each other about three different people.

5. Ask several pairs to demonstrate for the class.

### Practice 2

1. Have students read the directions.

2. Review the conversation from Practice 1, if necessary.

3. Give students time to think of how to describe other students in the class, for example:

   *Is (Mako) the one whose sister plays the piano?*

   *Is (Ken) the one whose relatives live in Toronto?*

   Tell students that they can ask and answer questions with true or false answers.

4. Pair Work. Have students take turns asking and answering questions about other students in the class.

5. Ask several pairs to demonstrate for the class.

### Extension

Ask each student in the class how they would like to be referred to, for example:

*I'm the young woman who likes animals.*

Tell them they can also make up something funny or interesting. Have each student tell the class once. Then have one student say *(Mariko) is the one who likes animals.* The next student describes *(Mariko)* and then another student in the class. Continue until one student can describe all the students in the class.

## Listen to This

Class CD 2, Track 38

### Part 1

1. Have students read the directions and look at the chart.

2. Play or read the conversation. Tell students to listen for the names of the three people that Adam and Gina are describing and write their names in the chart.

   A: This is a great apartment.

   G: I think so, too. Excuse me, but do I know you?

   A: No. I'm Adam. I came with Carl. I don't really know anyone here. Carl's told me about most of his friends, but I can't match the names with the faces.

   G: Well, let's see…OK, do you see that woman in the pink shirt?

   A: Yeah.

   G: That's Diana. She's the one who's moving to England next week. The party's for her.

   A: OK. And who's that guy?

   G: Which one?

   A: The one in the green chair.

   G: That's Cliff. He works in a bank.

   A: Oh! Is he the man who owns the racehorses?

   G: That's right. And do you see that guy with the beard?

   A: Uh-huh.

   G: That's Norm.

   A: Is he the one who owns the restaurant?

   G: No. Norm runs a dance studio. Let's see. Who else?

   A: Wait. I don't want to embarrass myself. Which one is the hostess? Her name is Gina, right?

   G: That's right. And I'm Gina. Nice to meet you. Glad you like my apartment!

3. Ask volunteers for the answers.

   > **Answers:**
   > Diana, Cliff, Norm

### Part 2

1. Have students read the directions.

2. Play or read the conversation again and tell students to listen for the information about each person mentioned.

3. Play or read the conversation again for students to check their answers.

4. Ask volunteers for their answers.

   > **Answers:**
   > Diana: in the pink shirt, moving to England next week, the party is for her
   > Cliff: in the green chair, works in a bank, owns the racehorses
   > Norm: with the beard, runs a dance studio

### Part 3

1. Have students read the directions.

2. Have students write a question to ask each of the three people described at the party. Brainstorm a few questions with the class, if necessary.

3. Group Work. Divide the students into groups of three. Have each student in the group choose one of the people described. Have the students take turns asking each other the questions they prepared for the person the other students are role-playing.

**Student Book page 83**

## Let's Talk

### Part 1

1. Have students read the directions and look at the examples.

2. Give students time to think of one interesting fact about themselves.

3. Group Work. Have one student in each group be the secretary and write down the sentence dictated by each student in the group. Ask the secretary to number the sentences.

### Part 2

1. Have students read the directions.

2. Group Work. Have groups switch papers and then discuss who they think each fact is about and why. Have the secretary write the guesses on a separate piece of paper and number them according to the sentences on the other group's paper.

3. Circulate and help as needed.

### Part 3

1. Have students read the directions.

2. Have groups switch the papers with the sentences and their guesses back and check the other group's guesses.

### Part 4

1. Have students read the directions.

2. Group Work. Have groups repeat the activities suggested in Parts 2 and 3 with each of the other groups in the class.

3. Class Work. When all groups are finished, have each group report the correct answers to the class. If time allows, have the class discuss why they made the guesses they did.

# What's she like?

## Vocabulary

Introduce these words and phrases to the students:

*semester:* period of school that usually lasts three or four months

*take (a class):* attend

*for one thing:* first of all (used to introduce a reason)

*Don't get me wrong:* Don't misunderstand me.

*pay attention:* to listen carefully

*not easy to talk to:* not easy to communicate with

## Prelistening

1. Have students open their books and look at the photograph. Ask:

   - *Where are the speakers?* (on a college campus)
   - *What do you think the girl is holding?* (a course catalog)

2. Pair Work. Read the title of the conversation and the prelistening question. Have students discuss the question in pairs.

3. Class Work. Have pairs share their answers with the class.

## Conversation 2

**Class CD 2, Track 39**

1. With books closed, play the recording or read the conversation.

   Mariko: Hi, Rosa. What are you doing?
   Rosa: I'm trying to pick an English literature class for this semester.
   Mariko: Take Professor Holt's class. I had her last year.
   Rosa: Really? What's she like?
   Mariko: Fantastic! I think she's a great teacher.
   Rosa: Why? What makes her so great?
   Mariko: For one thing, she's really funny.
   Rosa: Yeah, but I want to learn something.
   Mariko: Don't get me wrong. She's funny, and if someone's funny, you pay more attention. She's also really smart, so you learn a lot.
   Rosa: What do you think of Professor Vance?
   Mariko: He's boring. Everyone falls asleep in his class. And he's not very easy to talk to.
   Rosa: OK. I'll try to take Professor Holt's class.
   Mariko: I'm sure you'll enjoy it!

2. Ask these comprehension questions:

   - *What kind of class does Speaker 2 want to take?* (English literature)
   - *Whose class does Speaker 1 recommend?* (Professor Holt)

3. Say: *Listen again. This time listen for Speaker 1's opinion of the professors.*

4. Play or read the conversation again, pausing for choral repetition. Allow students to write down the information as they listen. Play or read the conversation again, if needed, for students to get all the information.

5. Ask the following questions:

   - *When did Speaker 1 take Professor Holt's class?* (last year)
   - *Why did Speaker 1 like Professor Holt?* (She's funny and smart.)
   - *What does Speaker 1 think of Professor Vance?* (He's boring.)
   - *Does she like to talk to him?* (No, he isn't easy to talk to.)
   - *What does Speaker 2 decide to do?* (take Professor Holt's class)

Elicit responses from various students.

## PRONUNCIATION FOCUS

**Class CD 2, Track 40**

1. Explain what the focus is. Play or read the examples in the book and have students repeat chorally.

   | | |
   |---|---|
   | learn | literature |
   | smart | professor |
   | year | teacher |

2. With books open, play or read the conversation again. Tell students to pay attention to the [r] sound after a vowel.

3. Paired Reading. Have students practice the conversation, switching roles.

## Give It a Try

# 1. Asking what someone is like

## Presentation

1. Have students look at the function box. Give them time to read the examples.

2. Model the exchanges in the function box and have students repeat chorally.

3. Practice a few exchanges with various students.

### Notes

1. Review the intonation of Wh- questions. On the board, write:

*What's she like?*

*What do you think of Professor Vance?*

Model the questions and have students repeat.

2. Explain that *What's he/she like?* asks for an opinion or information about the person's personality. *What does he/she look like?* asks for information about the person's appearance.

3. *He/She is funny* shows the speaker knows this from personal experience. *He/She seems funny* shows the speaker has an impression not necessarily based on personal experience with that person.

## Practice 1

1. Have students read the directions and look at the list and the chart. Go over vocabulary, if necessary.

2. Pair Work. Have students discuss if each quality is positive or negative. Explain that some of the qualities might be positive or negative depending on the situation or on the student's personal values. Have students explain their opinions.

3. Have students think of more adjectives and add them to the list. Have pairs compare their lists of new words.

4. Have pairs share their lists with the rest of the class.

## Practice 2

Class CD 2, Track 41

1. Have students read the directions and look at the chart and the words in the box.

2. Play or read the example conversation twice.

   A: What do you think of Professor Vance?
   B: He's boring.

3. Give students time to think of a famous person and four adjectives to describe him or her. Have students write the person's name and qualities in the chart.

4. Group Work. Divide students into groups of three or four. Have each group discuss each other's famous person and give their own opinions about what he or she is like.

5. Class Work. Have groups report their discussions to the class.

## Extension

1. Have students use their dictionaries to add words to the **Use These Words** list.

2. Have students write down four or five adjectives that describe their own personalities, but not write their names. Collect the papers. Read a paper and have the rest of the class guess who the person is.

## 2. Discussing qualities

### *Presentation*

1. Have students look at the function box. Give them time to read the examples.

2. Model the exchanges and have students repeat chorally.

3. Practice a few exchanges with various students.

### Note

The simple present tense is used in the result clause of a conditional statement to express a predictable fact. For example:

*If someone is funny, you <u>pay</u> more attention.*

Another way to express a conditional is to use the conjunction *so* to connect the two independent clauses. This expresses a relationship of *therefore* or *as a result*. For example:

*She's smart, <u>so</u> you pay more attention.*

### *Practice 1*

1. Have students read the directions and look at the words.

2. Give students time to think of someone they like and check off the qualities that describe them.

### *Practice 2*

**Class CD 2, Track 42**

1. Have students read the directions.

2. Play or read the example conversation twice.

   A: My friend is great!
   B: What makes her so great?
   A: She's smart, so you can learn a lot from her.

3. Pair Work. Have students discuss the people they chose in Practice 1.

4. Have several pairs demonstrate for the class.

### *Extension*

Have students create an adjectives dictionary. Tell them to make a list of adjectives and write a definition and the name of a person who has that particular quality.

## Listen to This

**Class CD 2, Track 43**

### Part 1

1. Have students read the directions.

2. Play or read the conversation. Tell students to listen for what the gift was and why the boy was unhappy about it.

   B: I'm really mad at Mom and Dad.
   G: Why? What did they do?
   B: I asked them for a leather jacket for my birthday, and they just got me this stupid raincoat.
   G: Oh, come on! It's a great coat.
   B: I don't care! I wanted leather.
   G: You know leather is expensive. Maybe they didn't have enough money.
   B: I want to return it and get leather! All my friends have leather jackets.
   G: They don't *all* have leather jackets.
   B: Anyway, on your birthday, Mom and Dad gave you what you asked for.
   G: That's true, but all I asked for was a new pair of jeans.
   B: I hate this raincoat.
   G: All right, how much is a leather jacket?
   B: If I return this raincoat, all I need is another $50.00.
   G: OK, I'll lend you the $50.00, but you have to pay me back.
   B: Great. Thank you so much, Sis!

3. Ask volunteers for the answers.

> **Answers:**
> A raincoat. He wanted a leather jacket.

### Part 2

1. Have students read the directions and look at the chart.

2. Play or read the conversation again and tell students to describe the boy's and girl's personalities.

3. Ask volunteers for their answers.

> **Possible Answers:**
> Boy:  selfish, ungrateful, envious
> Girl:  nice, understanding, appreciative, helpful

**Part 3**

1. Have students read the directions.

2. Pair Work. Have students discuss their answers and whether their adjectives are positive, negative, or both.

3. Have pairs report their discussion to the class.

### Extension

Class Discussion. Ask students to think of adjectives that can be both positive and negative. Make a list on the board. Discuss with the class when and how each adjective can be positive or negative.

**Student Book pages 87 & 113**

## Person to Person

**Part 1**

1. Divide the class into pairs and have students decide who will be Student A and who will be Student B. Remind Students B to look at page 113.

2. Have students read the directions and look at the list of words and the chart.

3. To check comprehension, read Student A's sentence 1 and ask:

   Student A, *what adjective describes this person?*

   Read Student B's sentence 1 and ask:

   Student B, *what adjective describes this person?*

4. Have students write an appropriate adjective next to each sentence. Circulate and help as needed.

**Part 2**

1. Have students read the directions.

2. Pair Work. Have students take turns reading the statements on their charts. Tell students to match the statements that could have been said by the same person.

3. Have several pairs share their answers with the class.

**Part 3**

1. Have students read the directions and look at the pictures.

2. Give students time to think of which person from Part 1 would be right for each job.

3. Pair Work. Have students talk about each of the jobs on their lists and what kind of people do each job. Have students discuss which person from Parts 1 and 2 would be right for each job.

4. Have pairs report their discussions to the class.

## Now Try This

1. Have students read the directions.

2. Give students time to think of which statements from Part 1 are true for them.

3. Pair Work. Have students take turns talking about which statements are true for them and asking advice about what job would be good for them.

4. Have several students report their partner's recommendations to the class.

# Unit 11  Have you ever tried it?

## Components

Student Book, pages 88–95
Class CD 2, Tracks 44–54
Optional Activities 11.1–11.2,
page 111

## Objectives

**Functions:** Discussing experiences, telling a story, responding to someone's story

**Topics:** Hobbies, leisure activities, reactions, past experiences

**Structures:** Present perfect, simple past, past continuous, time clauses with *when*

**Pronunciation Focus:** Past-tense ending *-ed*

**Listen to This:** Listening for specific information: descriptions of sports, adjectives; matching pictures and information from conversations

---

**Student Book page 88**

## CONSIDER THIS

1. Have students read the FAQs and answers and the last question. Go over vocabulary students don't know.

2. Group Work. Divide students into groups of three or four. Have students in each group answer the question and explain why they would like or not like to skysurf. Help students with vocabulary as needed.

3. Ask volunteers for their answers.

### Vocabulary

Introduce these words and phrases to the students:

*I'll say.*: I agree.

*gear*: equipment

*You're kidding.*: You're not serious. Really?

*really cool*: an informal way to say that something is very interesting

### Prelistening

1. Pair Work. Have students open their books and look at the photograph. Read the title of the conversation and the prelistening questions. Have students discuss what kind of sports equipment they can see in the picture and the kind of sports they like. Circulate and help with vocabulary as needed.

2. Ask volunteers to answer the questions.

## Conversation 1

**Class CD 2, Track 44**

1. With books closed, play the recording or read the conversation.

| | |
|---|---|
| Max: | Look at this equipment! I think there's something for every winter sport here. |
| Shigeo: | I'll say! Look at this snowboarding gear. Have you ever tried snowboarding? |
| Max: | Snowboarding? No, I've never done it. Have you? |
| Shigeo: | I tried it once. |
| Max: | You're kidding. When? |
| Shigeo: | Last year when I went to Korea. |
| Max: | What was it like? Was it fun? |
| Shigeo: | Oh, yeah. I fell down a lot at first. But it was really cool. |
| Max: | Did you try any other sports there? |
| Shigeo: | Yeah, we did some rock climbing. Have you ever done that? |
| Max: | Lots of times. I used to go every weekend. The last time was in the spring. I fell and hurt my leg. |
| Shigeo: | That's too bad. How about bungee-jumping? That's really scary. |
| Max: | Now that's something I *don't* want to try! |

2. Ask these comprehension questions:

- *Where are the speakers?* (in a sports shop)
- *What are they talking about?* (sports they have and haven't tried)

88  Unit 11

3. Play or read the conversation again, pausing for choral repetition.

4. Ask the following questions:

   - *Has Speaker 1 tried snowboarding?* (no)
   - *Where did Speaker 2 try snowboarding?* (in Korea)
   - *What happened to Speaker 2 when he went snowboarding?* (He fell down a lot at first, but he enjoyed it.)
   - *What other sports did Speaker 2 try?* (rock climbing)
   - *Has Speaker 1 ever done rock climbing?* (yes)
   - *Have the speakers tried bungee-jumping?* (no)

   Elicit responses from various students.

5. Paired Reading. Have students read the conversation, switching roles.

**Student Book page 89**

## Give It a Try

## 1. Discussing experiences (1)

### *Presentation*

1. Have students look at the function box. Give them time to read the examples.

2. Model the exchanges and have students repeat chorally.

3. Practice a few exchanges with various students.

### Note
Explain that *Have you ever (tried snowboarding)?* is used to ask if someone has done the action at any time in their life up until this moment.

### *Practice 1*

Class CD 2, Track 45

1. Have students read the directions and look at the pictures and the captions. Go over vocabulary, if necessary.

2. Play or read the example conversation twice.

   A: Have you ever tried snowboarding?
   B: Yes, I have.
   A: When?
   B: I've done it lots of times.

3. Pair Work. Have students take turns asking their partners if they have done any of the activities in the pictures.

4. Ask several pairs to demonstrate for the class.

### *Practice 2*

1. Have students read the directions.

2. Pair Work. Have students take turns finding out when their partners did any of the activities in Practice 1.

3. Ask several pairs to demonstrate for the class.

## 2. Discussing experiences (2)

### *Presentation*

1. Have students look at the function box. Give them time to read the examples.

2. Model the exchanges and have students repeat chorally.

### *Practice*

Class CD 2, Track 46

1. Have students read the directions and look at the list of activities. Go over vocabulary, if necessary.

2. Give students time to think of their own activities to ask about.

3. Play or read the example conversation twice.

   A: Have you ever tried mountain climbing?
   B: Yes, I've done it lots of times.
   A: When was the last time you went mountain climbing?
   B: The last time was in the spring. I fell and hurt my leg.

4. Pair Work. Have students take turns asking about the last time their partners did any of the activities listed.

5. Ask several pairs to demonstrate for the class.

# 3. Discussing experiences (3)

Review. Say an activity such as: *skydiving*. Point to a student and elicit the question *Have you ever tried skydiving?* Have another student in the class answer the question. Give that student a different prompt and have them ask the question to a different student. Continue the activity as time allows.

## Presentation

1. Have students look at the function box. Give them time to read the examples.

2. Model the exchanges and have students repeat chorally.

3. Have some pairs practice a few exchanges with different combinations.

## Notes

1. In order to help students distinguish the description of an activity (*It was exciting.*) from someone's reaction to it (*I was excited.*), write on the board:

   *The movie was scary.*

   *I was scared.*

   Model and have students repeat. Continue, using sentences with *terrifying* and *terrified*, *interesting* and *interested*, etc. Then give students prompts and have them make their own sentences.

2. Review the intonation of statements with *but*. Point out that in each statement joined by *but*, there is at least one strong stress, each accompanied by a rising and falling intonation. On the board, write the following and mark the intonation:

   *I was terrified, but I loved it.*

   Model the sentences and have students repeat.

## Practice 1

**Class CD 2, Track 47**

1. Have students read the directions and look at the words in the box. Go over vocabulary, if necessary.

2. Play or read the example conversation twice.

   A: I tried snowboarding last winter.
   B: Really? What was it like?
   A: I was terrified at first.

3. Give students time to think of interesting sports and activities they have tried.

4. Pair Work. Have students take turns asking each other about activities they have done and how they felt about it.

5. Ask several pairs to demonstrate for the class.

## Practice 2

1. Have students read the directions and look at the chart.

2. Give students time to write the names of three sports under each category. Brainstorm sports and activities as a class, if necessary.

3. Pair Work. Have students discuss their charts and if they agree with their partner's choices.

4. Ask several pairs to report their discussion to the class.

## Listen to This

**Class CD 2, Track 48**

### Part 1

1. Have students read the directions and look at the pictures. Identify the sports in the pictures with the class, if necessary.

2. Play or read the accounts. Tell students to write the number of the correct account next to each picture.

   **1**
   You need to go somewhere where there's a fair bit of wind. Most people start with a two-liner. We spent hours running up and down the beach with it first, and then when we finally got to go out onto the water, I got the lines tangled up right away. Once you're up on your feet it's fine, but it took me about two hours the first time I tried it. It was very frustrating. I spent more time in the water than on the board! I was totally exhausted.

   **2**
   You need to go up somewhere really high. You never get tired of that wonderful feeling when you lift off and you're suspended in the air, thousands of feet above land with nothing but the sound of a gentle breeze. You feel so calm and peaceful. It's exhilarating. There's nothing like it!

   **3**
   You have to get up somewhere really high like a bridge or a tower. Or people sometimes use helicopters or hot air balloons. You have a body harness on. There's a bunch of cords attached to your middle. And then you jump! If you're lucky, you can get two or three really good bounces. Scary? You bet! It scared the life out of me! Terrific!

3. Ask volunteers for the answers.

**Answers:** 1, 3, 2

## Part 2

1. Have students read the directions.

2. Play or read the accounts again and tell students to listen for the key words that helped them identify each sport.

3. Play or read the conversations again for students to check their answers.

4. Ask volunteers for their answers.

**Answers:**

| | |
|---|---|
| kite surfing: | wind, beach, water, board |
| hang gliding: | high, lift off, suspended in the air, thousands of feet above land |
| bungee jumping: | high, body harness, jump, bounces |

## Part 3

1. Have students read the directions.

2. Have students write how each person felt. Play or read the accounts again, if necessary.

3. Ask volunteers for their answers.

**Answers:**

| | |
|---|---|
| kite surfing: | it was frustrating, he was exhausted |
| hang gliding: | he was calm and peaceful, it was exhilarating |
| bungee jumping: | he was scared, but it was terrific |

## Let's Talk

### Part 1

1. Have students read the directions and look at the pictures and the chart.

2. Give students time to think of five sports they have tried and one adjective to describe them. Tell them to write the sports, when they tried each one, and the adjectives in the chart.

### Part 2

1. Have students read the directions.

2. Class Work. Have students walk around the classroom and ask other students if they have tried the same sports. When they find someone who has tried the same sport or sports, have them take turns asking when they did it and their opinion of it. Tell students to write the answers in their chart.

3. Circulate and help as needed.

### Part 3

1. Have students read the directions.

2. Class Work. Have students tell the class if they would recommend the sports in their chart to anyone else and why or why not.

3. Have a class vote on the most popular sport.

# I'll never forget the time I...

Student Book page 92

## Vocabulary

Introduce these phrases to the students:

*handed it to*: gave it to

*got off (the train)*: left (the train)

*get home*: return home

*did laundry*: washed clothes

## Prelistening

1. Have students open their books and look at the photograph. Ask:

   • *Where are the speakers?* (on a train/subway)
   • *Where do you think they're going?* (to do some kind of sports)

2. Pair Work. Divide the class into pairs. Read the title of the conversation and the prelistening question. Have the partners discuss the question.

3. Have pairs share their answers with the class.

### Notes

1. Train stations usually have a "lost and found" where people hand in items left on the train. If someone thinks they left something on the train, they can ask if anyone handed the item into the lost and found.

2. Review the usage of phrasal verbs such as *get on, get off, get out, pick up,* and *pick out.*

## Conversation 2

**Class CD 2, Track 49**

1. With books closed, play the recording or read the conversation.

   Shigeo: Did I ever tell you about the time I found some money on the train?
   Max: No. What happened?
   Shigeo: I was taking the train to my judo class, when I saw a wallet on the seat next to me. I picked it up, and it had about $150 in it.
   Max: What did you do? Did you keep the money?
   Shigeo: No. I handed it to a police officer when I got off.
   Max: Good for you. That was really honest of you.
   Shigeo: I had a nice surprise three months later. They called me and gave me the money. They couldn't find the person who lost it.
   Max: Well, I'll never forget the time I lost money.
   Shigeo: Oh, no. Was it a lot?

   Max: I was on the train when I realized I had forgotten my train pass. I took out my wallet to pay for the ticket and my wallet was empty! I was sure I had about $100.
   Shigeo: So what did you do about the ticket? How did you get home?
   Max: Oh, I had to get out at the next station and walk! I went home and I searched everywhere.
   Shigeo: Did you ever find it?
   Max: You won't believe it. I found it the next time I did laundry. It was in my pants' pocket the whole time.

2. Ask these comprehension questions:

   • *What did Speaker 1 find on the train?* (money)
   • *What did he do with the money?* (gave it to a police officer)
   • *What happened three months later? Why?* (He got the money back because they couldn't find the person who lost it.)

3. Say: *Listen again. This time listen for what happened to Speaker 2.*

4. Play or read the conversation again, pausing for choral repetition. Allow students to write down the information as they listen. Play or read the conversation again, if needed, for students to get all the information.

5. Ask the following questions:
   - *What did Speaker 2 lose?* (money)
   - *What did he forget?* (his train pass)
   - *What happened when he took out his wallet?* (He realized it was empty.)
   - *How much money did he think he had?* ($100)
   - *How did he get home?* (He got out at the next station and walked home.)
   - *Where did he find the money?* (in his pants' pocket)

Elicit responses from various students.

## PRONUNCIATION FOCUS
**Class CD 2, Track 50**

1. Explain what the focus is. Write the examples on the board and add some of the other verbs ending in *-ed* in the conversation under the correct column. Play or read the examples in the book and have students repeat chorally.

   [t]:  picked
   [d]:  called
   [id]:  handed

2. With books open, play or read the conversation again. Tell students to pay attention to the pronunciation of the final *-ed* of the words.

3. Paired Reading. Have students practice the conversation, switching roles.

**Student Book page 93**

## Give It a Try

## 1. Telling a story

### Presentation

1. Have students look at the function box. Give them time to read the examples.

2. Model the exchanges and have students repeat chorally.

3. Practice a few exchanges with various students.

### Note
The past continuous and the simple past are often used to tell a story. The past continuous describes an action that was in progress some time in the past. It is often used to set the scene for the main action, which is usually expressed in the simple past. For example:

   I *was sitting* in a chair when I *heard* a loud crash.

### Practice 1
**Class CD 2, Track 51**

1. Have students read the directions and look at the pictures and the captions.

2. Play or read the example conversation twice.

   A: Did I ever tell you about the time I found $150?
   B: No. What happened?
   A: I was taking the train to my judo class, when I saw a wallet on the seat next to me.

3. Pair Work. Give students time to choose one of the pictures and think of a story. Have students take turns telling their story and asking questions about it.

4. Have several pairs demonstrate their conversations for the class.

### Practice 2
**Class CD 2, Track 52**

1. Have students read the directions.

2. Play or read the example conversation twice.

   A: I was taking the train to my judo class, when I saw a wallet on the seat next to me.
   B: What did you do?
   A: I gave it to a police officer when I got off.

3. Give students time to think of how to extend their story and what questions to ask about their partner's story.

4. Pair Work. Have students take turns telling their story and asking questions about their partner's story.

### Practice 3

1. Have students read the directions and look at the list.

2. Give students time to think of their own story.

3. Pair Work. Have students take turns telling their stories and asking questions about their partners' stories.

4. Have several pairs demonstrate their conversation to the class.

5. Have a class vote on who had the funniest or most interesting story.

### Extension

1. Have a longest story contest. Have pairs see who can have the longest conversation about a story. Set a time limit for pauses between questions and answers so that the story sounds natural. See which pair can keep their conversation going the longest.

2. Make a story circle. Have students sit in a circle. Say a sentence such as, *The other day I was at the park and heard a very strange noise.* Have the next student say a sentence that continues the story. Continue around the circle. As an alternative, have every third student ask a question about what was just said and the next student answer it.

## 2. Responding to someone's story

Review. Have one student say the first sentence of a story and another student ask a question about it. Have a third student answer it, continuing the story. Continue with other students.

### Presentation

1. Have students look at the function boxes. Give them time to read the examples.

2. Model the exchanges and have students repeat chorally.

3. Practice a few exchanges with various students.

### Note

Explain to students that asking questions and making comments about someone's story is a way to show that you are interested. Not asking questions can be interpreted as being bored and therefore can be a little impolite.

### Practice

**Class CD 2, Track 53**

1. Have students read the directions and look at the list and the expressions in the box.

2. Give students time to think of their own idea to add to the list.

3. Play or read the example conversation twice.

   A: I turned the wallet into the police.
   B: Good for you. That was really honest of you. Did they find the owner?

4. Pair Work. Have pairs take turns telling a story and asking questions about it.

5. Have several pairs demonstrate their conversation to the class. Have other students in the class ask other questions about the stories.

### Extension

Write several story beginnings on the board such as, *My brother was late to his own wedding.* Have students think of what questions they would ask about each story and write them on the board. Put students into groups and have them choose one of the stories on the board. Tell them to write a story based on the story beginning and the questions. Have each group present their story to the class.

## Listen to This

**Class CD 2, Track 54**

### Part 1

1. Have students read the directions.

2. Play or read the conversation. Tell students to write a title for the story.

   L: The most embarrassing thing that ever happened to me was a couple of years ago when I had just passed my driving test. I was driving through the city, very pleased and happy that I was driving on my own at last. There was quite a lot of traffic, but it wasn't too bad. In fact, the cars were moving very slowly which was fine for me. Then suddenly, the engine cut out.

   P: The car stopped?

   L: Yes! Well, I tried to start it up again, but I must have flooded the engine or something, because it just wouldn't start.

   P: Oh, no! What did you do then?

   L: I just didn't know what to do! I started to panic. I was in the middle of this really busy street, four lanes of traffic all around me, cars starting to line up behind me. I couldn't leave the car to go and get help. I just sat there, terrified.

   P: That sounds awful. How embarrassing. And then what happened?

   L: I suppose I was sitting there for at least ten minutes, but it seemed like an hour. And then a man came up out of the subway, saw what was happening, and came over to the car. And together we pushed the car over to the sidewalk, out of the way of the traffic. I was so relieved! I mean, he knew immediately what to do, and it was so simple, really.

   P: Wow! What did you say to him?

   L: Well, that was the funny thing. He couldn't speak any English, so I couldn't tell him how grateful I was. He just smiled and went away.

   P: And you never saw him again?

   L: No, I never saw him again.

3. Ask volunteers for their answers.

**Possible Answers:**
*Answers will vary.*
The Most Embarrassing Thing
I Started a Traffic Jam

### Part 2

1. Have students read the directions and look at the pictures.

2. Play or read the conversation again and tell students to listen for adjectives that describe Lisa's feelings at each part of the story.

3. Ask volunteers for their answers.

> **Possible Answers:**
> 1. pleased, happy
> 2. panicked, terrified
> 3. relieved, grateful

### Part 3

1. Have students read the directions.

2. Play or read the conversation again. Tell students to think of three questions to ask about the story.

3. Pair Work. Have students take turns asking each other questions about the story.

4. Have several pairs tell their questions and answers to the class.

**Student Book page 95**

## Person to Person

### Part 1

1. Have students read the directions and look at the list of questions.

2. Give students time to think of an unusual event and answer the questions about it. Tell students they can think of an untrue story as well.

3. Circulate and help as needed.

### Part 2

1. Have students read the directions and look at the top diagram.

2. Pair Work. Divide the class into groups of four. Have students decide who will be Student A, B, C, and D. Have Students A and B take turns telling their story and taking notes about their partner's story. Have Students C and D do the same.

### Part 3

1. Have students read the directions.

2. Pair Work. Have students change partners within their groups. Have students tell their previous partners' stories and take notes on the new story they hear.

## Now Try This

1. Have students read the directions and look at the diagram at the bottom of the page.

2. Group Work. Have each student tell the last story they heard to their group. Tell the other students to ask questions. Have the person who originally told the story check to make sure all the details are correct.

## Components

Student Book, pages 96–103, 114
Class CD 2, Tracks 55–65
Optional Activities 12.1–12.2, pages 111–112

## Objectives

**Functions:** Asking and giving opinions, agreeing and disagreeing with opinions, giving reasons, social issues, seeing the other side

**Topics:** Movies, TV shows, books

**Structures:** Simple past, *neither/so, too/either*, negative Wh-questions

**Pronunciation Focus:** Soft and hard [th] sounds

**Listen to This:** Listening for specific information: opinions and reasons; listening for gist: topics; filling in charts

---

**Student Book page 96**

## CONSIDER THIS

1. Have students read the text and the question. Go over vocabulary students don't know.
2. Class Work. Ask a student who his or her favorite movie star is and why. Ask the student to ask another student. Continue until all students had answered the question.

### *Vocabulary*

Introduce this phrase to the students:

*martial arts:* methods of fighting, such as karate and judo, usually practiced as sports and self-defense

### *Prelistening*

1. Pair Work. Have students open their books and look at the photograph. Have partners describe what they see to each other. Circulate and help with vocabulary as needed.
2. Read the title of the conversation and the prelistening questions.
3. Group Work. Divide students into groups of four or five. Have students discuss the questions.
4. Ask volunteers for their answers.

## Conversation 1

**Class CD 2, Track 55**

1. With books closed, play the recording or read the conversation.

   Angie: What did you think of the movie?
   John:   I thought it was great.
   Angie: You did? I thought it was terrible.
   John:   Why? What didn't you like about it?
   Angie: For one thing, it was too violent. There was too much fighting.
   John:   But, Angie, it was a martial arts movie!
   Angie: I know, but the story was silly, too.
   John:   The stories are always silly in those movies.
   Angie: Then why do you like them?
   John:   They're exciting and I like the fight scenes.
   Angie: Yeah, but the acting is terrible.
   John:   They don't have to act. They just have to know how to fight. It's like watching a dance.
   Angie: Then maybe we should go to the ballet next time!

2. Ask these comprehension questions:

   • *Where are the speakers?* (a movie theater)
   • *What kind of movie did they see?* (action/martial arts movie)

3. Play or read the conversation again, pausing for choral repetition.

4. Ask the following questions:

- *What did Speaker 1 think of the movie?* (that it was terrible)
- *What did Speaker 2 think of the movie?* (He thought it was great.)
- *What didn't Speaker 1 like about it?* (It was too violent, the story was silly, and the acting was terrible.)
- *What does Speaker 2 agree with?* (that the story was silly and that the acting was not good)
- *Why does Speaker 2 like martial arts movies?* (They're exciting and he likes fight scenes.)

Elicit responses from various students.

5. Paired Reading. Have students read the conversation, switching roles.

**Student Book page 97**

## Give It a Try

## 1. Asking and giving opinions

### Presentation

1. Have students look at the function box. Give them time to read the examples.

2. Model the exchanges and have students repeat chorally.

3. Have various pairs of students practice different combinations of the exchanges.

### Notes

1. In some cultures it is not customary to express strong opinions openly, especially with strangers. However, people in the United States generally value an open exchange of ideas, as long as the topic is not too personal and the speaker is careful in his or her choice of words and tone of voice. It is very important to sound respectful of the other person's opinions.

2. Review intonation of sentences that give an opinion. On the board, write the following sentences without the intonation or stress marked:

I *thought* it was *great*.

I *loved* it.

It was *terrible*.

Ask students which words they think will be stressed in these sentences. Mark the stress and the intonation. Model and have students repeat.

### Practice

**Class CD 2, Track 56**

1. Have students read the directions and look at the list of events.

2. Play or read the example conversation twice.

A: What did you think of the movie?
B: I thought it was great.

3. Pair Work. Have students take turns asking and answering questions about the events on the list.

4. Ask several pairs to demonstrate for the class.

## 2. Agreeing and disagreeing with opinions

### Presentation

1. Have students look at the function boxes. Give them time to read the examples.

2. Model the exchanges and have students repeat chorally.

3. Practice a few exchanges with various students.

### Notes

1. Review the structures to indicate agreement with *too, either, so* and *neither. Too* and *so* are used to indicate agreement with affirmative statements. *Either* and *neither* are used to indicate agreement with negative statements. *Too* and *either* are used at the end of the statements. *So* and *neither* are used at the beginning of the short statements and followed by the auxiliary verb and the subject. Notice that *neither* already has a negative meaning and is not followed by a negative verb.

A: I *loved* it.

B: I loved it, *too*.   or

  *So* did I.

A: I *didn't* like it.

B: I didn't like it *either*.   or

  *Neither* did I.

2. Explain to students that when a sentence with *think* is followed by another sentence, the negative form of it is in the sentence with the verb *think*:

I thought it was very good.

I didn't think it was very good.

and not ~~I thought it wasn't very good~~.

## Practice 1

Class CD 2, Track 57

1. Have students read the directions and look at the lists.

2. Have students decide who will be Student A and who will be Student B. Give students time to think of examples for each of the items on their list.

3. Play or read the example conversation twice.

   A: What did you think of the movie?
   B: I thought it was great.
   A: So did I.

4. Pair Work. Have students take turns asking each other's opinion about each item on their list.

5. Ask several pairs to demonstrate for the class.

## Practice 2

1. Have students read the directions.

2. Have students walk around the classroom and ask other students their opinion about the items from Practice 1. Make sure students agree or disagree with the other students' opinions.

**Student Book page 98**

## 3. Giving reasons

Review. Give a prompt such as: *the new (Steven Spielberg) movie*. Point to a student and elicit their opinion. Point to another student and have them agree or disagree. Continue with other prompts. Move quickly around the classroom.

### Presentation

1. Have students look at the function boxes. Give them time to read the examples.

2. Model the exchanges and have students repeat chorally.

3. Practice a few exchanges with various students.

## Practice 1

Class CD 2, Track 58

1. Have students read the directions and look at the list and words in the box. Go over vocabulary, if necessary.

2. Play or read the example conversation twice.

   A: What did you think of the movie?
   B: I thought it was terrible.
   A: What didn't you like about it?
   B: It was too violent.

3. Pair Work. Give students time to think of a movie they have both seen. Have students take turns asking each other their opinions about the aspects of the movie mentioned.

4. Ask several pairs to demonstrate for the class.

## Practice 2

1. Have students read the directions.

2. Pair Work. Give students time to think of a TV show they have both seen. Have students take turns asking each other their opinions about the aspects of the TV show mentioned.

3. Ask several pairs to demonstrate for the class.

## Practice 3

1. Have students read the directions.

2. Pair Work. Give students time to think of a book they have both read. Have students take turns asking each other their opinions about the aspects of the book mentioned.

3. Ask several pairs to demonstrate for the class.

## Extension

1. Have students use their dictionary to add words to the **Use These Words** list.

2. If there is a book, movie, or TV show that all of the students know, have a class discussion about it. Make sure all students give their opinions.

## Listen to This

Class CD 2, Track 59

### Part 1

1. Have students read the directions and look at the chart.

2. Play or read the conversation. Tell students to put a √ or an X in the chart.

   N: Welcome to another edition of *The Critical Eye*. Tonight, Jean Lovitt and Henry Pandit will give you their opinions on movies that will be opening soon in movie theaters across America.
   H: Good evening, Jean.
   J: Good evening, Henry. The first movie we're going to talk about tonight is *The Final Chapter*. Of course, I don't want to reveal too much, but it involves politics, murder, and a writer who uncovers some deadly secrets. This movie has everything—mystery, suspense, romance, and action. The problem is, the movie just doesn't work.
   H: Why didn't you like it? I thought it was a great story. It kept my attention. There were a lot of details to remember, but it never got confusing. I thought the story was excellent.
   J: You did? I didn't. I thought there were too many details. I found it really slow-moving and frustrating. I mean, they didn't need the romance between the detective and the writer.

H: That's true, but I think they wanted the characters to have more personality. I liked the characters more because of the romance.

J: Well, I didn't really like them because their relationship was just too slow-moving and boring. But, I thought the acting was good. Sam Foster's character was so real. I really liked his acting.

H: You did? I didn't. He was just OK. I really thought newcomer Cassie Lane, as the writer, was a bore! It's too bad—two good characters almost ruined by two bad acting jobs.

J: Well, I have to say, don't waste your money on this movie! The story is confusing and the characters are silly. Good acting couldn't save it!

H: And I say, the acting isn't that great, but the story and the characters are good enough to keep you entertained.

J: Now it's up to you. You've heard our opinions.

H: Now the final decision is yours.

3. Ask volunteers for the answers.

> **Answers:**
> Jean: didn't like the story or the characters; liked the acting
> Henry: liked the story, the characters; didn't like the acting

### Part 2

1. Have students read the directions.

2. Play or read the conversation again and tell students to listen for the reasons the reviewers give for liking or not liking each aspect of the movie.

3. Play or read the conversation again for students to check their answers.

4. Ask volunteers for their answers.

> **Answers:**
> Jean: the story had too many details, it was slow-moving and frustrating; the characters' relationship was too slow-moving and boring, the characters were silly; the acting was good, Sam Foster's character was so real
> Henry: the story kept his attention, it was not confusing; the romance made the characters more likable, the characters had more personality; the acting wasn't good, Sam Foster was just OK, Cassie Lane was a bore

### Part 3

1. Have students read the directions.

2. Play or read the conversation again, if necessary.

3. Ask volunteers for their answers.

> **Answers:**
> Jean did not recommend it; Henry did.

**Student Book page 99**

## Let's Talk

### Part 1

1. Have students read the directions.

2. Group Work. Divide the students into groups of three or four. Give students time to think of four movies they have all seen and write them down.

### Part 2

1. Have students read the directions and look at the chart.

2. Have students write their individual opinions about each movie in each category.

3. Circulate and help as needed.

### Part 3

1. Have students read the directions.

2. Group Work. Have each group from Part 1 discuss their opinions for each category. Make sure they talk about why they agree or disagree with each other. Then have them vote on which of the movies is the most popular.

### Part 4

1. Have students read the directions.

2. Class Work. Have a member from each group write their winning movie on the board and then tell the class why the group voted it as the best. Encourage the other students to say if they disagree and why. When all groups have finished, have the class vote on the best film.

### Extension

If time allows, repeat this process with different groups. This time have them talk about TV shows.

# If you ask me...

## *Vocabulary*

Introduce these words and phrases to the students:

*to sit through it*: to watch the whole thing

*harmful*: dangerous

*if you ask me*: in my opinion

*take seriously*: to care a lot about

*nowadays*: in recent times

*social problems*: problems in the interaction/relationship with other people in society

*superficial*: without real or serious content

## *Prelistening*

1. Have students open their books and look at the photograph. Ask:

   - *Where are the speakers?* (in a restaurant)
   - *What kind of conversation do you think they are having?* (a discussion about a movie)

2. Pair Work. Read the title of the conversation and the prelistening questions. Have students discuss the questions with their partners.

3. Have pairs share their answers with the class.

### Note
Remind students that body language, facial expressions, word choice, and intonation are very important when discussing opinions, especially with someone you don't know well. Explain that it is imperative to appear respectful of others' opinions.

## Conversation 2

**Class CD 2, Track 60**

1. With books closed, play the recording or read the conversation.

   Angie: That movie was so violent—it was hard for me to sit through it! What do you think about violence in movies? Do you think it's harmful?

   John: I don't think violence in movies is that bad.

   Angie: Well, if you ask me, I think it is a problem. Kids grow up thinking that it's OK to hurt people.

   John: Oh, come on! I think people worry too much about violence on TV and in the movies. It's not something kids take seriously. I don't think it affects their behavior.

   Angie: Oh, no? Then why is it that kids nowadays are so aggressive and have so many social problems in school?

   John: Well, personally, I think romantic movies with happy endings are silly. They give people unrealistic expectations.

   Angie: That's true. They are superficial and they don't deal with real-life issues at all. But at least they don't encourage people to commit crimes and kill each other.

2. Ask these comprehension questions:

   - *Are the speakers agreeing or disagreeing about something?* (disagreeing)
   - *What do they disagree about?* (violence in movies)

3. Say: *Listen again. This time listen for the details of the conversation.*

4. Play or read the conversation again, pausing for choral repetition. Allow students to write down the information as they listen. Play or read the conversation again, if needed, for students to get all the information.

5. Ask the following questions:

- *Does Speaker 2 think violence in movies is harmful?* (no)
- *What effect does Speaker 1 think violence in movies has on children?* (Children think it's OK to hurt people.)
- *Does Speaker 2 agree? Why or why not?* (No. He thinks kids don't take it seriously.)
- *What does Speaker 2 think about romantic movies?* (They are silly and give people unrealistic expectations.)
- *Does Speaker 1 agree that they are silly?* (yes)
- *Does Speaker 1 think romantic movies are harmful?* (no)

Elicit responses from various students.

## PRONUNCIATION FOCUS

**Class CD 2, Track 61**

1. Explain what the focus is. Play or read the examples in the book and have students repeat chorally, noticing the different pronunciation of [th] in the words.

| | |
|---|---|
| through | that |
| think | they |
| something | then |

2. With books open, play or read the conversation again. Tell students to pay attention to the two sounds of [th].

3. Paired Reading. Have students practice the conversation, switching roles.

**Student Book page 101**

## Give It a Try

## 1. Asking and giving opinions

### Presentation

1. Have students look at the function box. Give them time to read the examples.

2. Model the exchanges and have students repeat chorally.

3. Practice a few exchanges with various students.

### Practice

**Class CD 2, Track 62**

1. Have students read the directions and look at the list and the words in the box. Go over any vocabulary students don't know.

2. Play or read the example conversation twice.

A: What do you think about violence in movies?
B: Well, if you ask me, I think it is a problem.
A: I agree. Kids grow up thinking that it's OK to hurt people.
B: I think so, too.

3. Pair Work. Give students time to choose one of the types of TV shows or use their own idea and think about their opinion. Have students take turns asking and giving their opinion about the types of TV shows.

4. Have several pairs demonstrate their conversations for the class.

## 2. Agreeing and adding a reason

### Presentation

1. Have students look at the function box. Give them time to read the examples.

2. Model the exchanges and have students repeat chorally.

3. Practice a few exchanges with various students.

### Practice

**Class CD 2, Track 63**

1. Have students read the directions and look at the list.

2. Play or read the example conversation twice.

A: Personally, I think romantic movies with happy endings are silly. They give people unrealistic expectations.
B: That's true. They're so superficial. They don't deal with real-life issues at all.

3. Give students time to think of their opinions about each of the topics and add their own ideas. Brainstorm opinions a person could have about each topic, if necessary.

4. Pair Work. Have students take turns giving an opinion and a reason and agreeing with it and adding a reason.

5. Have several pairs demonstrate their conversations for the class.

## Extension

1. Have students practice giving opinions in different situations with different people. For example, ask students to imagine that they hated a movie. Ask them to role-play how they would give their opinion to a member of their family, to an acquaintance at a dinner party, and to their boss or their teacher at a party at the office or at the school. Brainstorm other opinions and situations and role-play them. Make sure students pay attention to their tone and their body language.

2. If any of the topics on the page were particularly popular to talk about, organize a formal debate about it. Have some students be on the pro side, some students be on the con side, and the rest of the students judge which side made the best argument. Give students time to write down and organize their reasons, and to plan how they will present their argument.

Student Book page 102

## 3. Seeing the other side

### Presentation

1. Have students look at the function box. Give them time to read the examples.

2. Model the exchanges and have students repeat chorally.

3. Practice a few exchanges with various students.

### Note
The phrases:

*That's true, but...*

*I see your point, but...*

*I know what you mean, but...*

are often used to soften an expression of disagreement. The speaker first acknowledges the other person's opinion before disagreeing.

### Practice

Class CD 2, Track 64

1. Have students read the directions and look at the pictures. Identify the topic in each picture, if necessary.

2. Play or read the example conversation twice.

A: I think romantic movies with happy endings are silly. They give people unrealistic expectations.

B: That's true, but at least they don't encourage people to commit crimes and kill each other.

3. Pair Work. Give students time to think of their opinion about the topic in each picture. Have pairs take turns giving an opinion and disagreeing.

4. Have several pairs demonstrate their conversation to the class. Have other students in the class think of other possible reasons to disagree with each opinion.

## Listen to This

Class CD 2, Track 65

### Part 1

1. Have students read the directions and look at the chart.

2. Play or read the conversations. Tell students to write the topics being discussed.

**1**
M: I see in the paper they're sending another rocket to Mars.
W: Oh, great. How much is that going to cost?
M: Oh, a couple million, I guess.
W: Well, I think it's a big waste of money! There are poor countries and people starving on this planet. I think these space flights are stupid.
M: I don't think so. Because of them we have TV and weather satellites. Besides, we might have to live there some day.
W: Not me! I'm staying right here.

**2**
M: Your dog was barking all day yesterday. You shouldn't leave him at home like that.
W: That's only because my mother went out for the day. Usually he's a very quiet dog.
M: I don't agree with keeping pets. Especially when you live in apartments as small as ours. It's not good for animals to be in a small space like that. They need to run around in the fresh air.
W: Our dog is very happy at home with us. He has a very nice life! Only the best food, and lots of love and attention from me and my Mom!
M: I suppose he keeps your mother company....
W: Yes, and it's good exercise for her when she takes him for a walk.
M: Well, I guess it's OK.... Just try not to leave him alone all day again, OK?

3. Ask volunteers for the answers.

> **Answers:**
> 1. sending rockets to Mars
> 2. keeping pets (in an apartment)

## Part 2

1. Have students read the directions.

2. Play or read the conversations again and tell students to listen for each speaker's opinion about the topics.

3. Play the conversations again for students to check their answers.

4. Ask volunteers for their answers.

**Answers:**

1. Man: space travel leads to important innovations like TV and weather satellites, and we may need to live on another planet some day

   Woman: space flights are a waste of money because the money could be spent on helping people

2. Man: animals should not be kept in small apartments or left alone all day, they need to run around in the fresh air

   Woman: pets in apartments can have a nice life and it can be good exercise when you walk them

## Part 3

1. Have students read the directions.

2. Group Work. Have students discuss additional arguments for each topic in groups.

3. Class Work. Have each group present their arguments to the class. Have students vote on the most popular opinions for each topic.

### Extension

Brainstorm other topics for discussion. Have the class vote on the most interesting and/or important topic. Have a class discussion about that topic.

**Student Book pages 103 & 114**

## Person to Person

### Part 1

1. Divide the class into pairs and have students decide who will be Student A and who will be Student B. Remind Students B to look at page 114.

2. Have students read the instructions and look at their surveys. Go over vocabulary, if necessary.

3. Give students time to write if they agree or disagree with each statement and answer the question.

4. Circulate and help as needed.

## Part 2

1. Have students read the directions.

2. Pair Work. Have Student A interview Student B. To check comprehension, ask:

   *Student (A, B), what is one question you will ask Student (B, A)?*

   Have students take turns interviewing each other and agreeing or disagreeing with each other. Make sure students take notes of each other's answers.

### Part 3

1. Have students read the directions.

2. Give students time to summarize their partner's opinions and reasons for them.

3. Class Work. Have each student report on his or her partner's opinions.

### Now Try This

1. Have students read the directions.

2. Pair Work. Have each pair think of another topic and create a survey. Have the pairs exchange surveys with another pair.

3. Pair Work. Using the other pair's survey, have students take turns interviewing their partners.

4. Class Work. Have the pairs summarize the results of their surveys to the class.

### Extension

Bring in articles that express opinions about a particular topic. Have each student read one of the articles and summarize the writer's opinion for the class. Have the class discuss if they agree or disagree with the writer's opinion and why.

## Components

Student Book, pages 104–105
Class CD 2, tracks 66–68

**Student Book page 104**

## Listen To This Unit 10

**Class CD 2, Track 66**

1. Have students read the directions and look at the chart and the list of adjectives.

2. Play or read the conversations.

**1**
M: What a terrible waitress. No tip for her.
W: Well, I'm going to tip her. It's a tough job, especially at lunchtime. I used to be a waitress, so I know.

**2**
W: Our computer teacher is really boring. I'm sure I could teach better than that!
M: Oh yeah, since when are you an expert on computers?
W: I could teach a computer class if I wanted to!
M: You don't know what you're talking about! I'm glad I'm not in your class!

**3**
W: Hi! I'm Lisa! Are you a new student!
M: Yes…it's my first day…and I don't know anyone here.
W: Oh, I know everyone! And I've only been here two days. You'll soon make friends, don't worry. I'll introduce you to everyone I know!
M: That's really very kind of you. Thanks a lot.

3. Have students fill in the chart.

4. Play or read the conversations again for students to check their answers.

5. Ask volunteers for their answers.

> **Answers:**
> 1. Man: rude, stingy
>    Woman: considerate, supportive
> 2. Man: conceited, confident
>    Woman: aggressive, rude
> 3. Man: shy, polite
>    Woman: friendly, considerate, outgoing

## Give It a Try

1. Have students read the directions and look at page 81.

2. Pair Work. Have students take turns choosing someone from page 81 and guessing who it is.

3. Have several pairs demonstrate for the class.

## Listen To This Unit 11

**Class CD 2, Track 67**

1. Have students read the directions and look at the chart. Make sure students understand each question.

2. Play or read the story.

This happened to me about four years ago in the summer. I was driving home from work one night. It was about eight in the evening. It was just getting dark. There was a beautiful sunset. I'd had a very difficult day at work, and I was looking forward to a nice relaxing evening at home.

I looked up at the sky, and I saw this string of bright lights. It looked like a group of airplanes. But I couldn't hear anything, and they were moving very slowly. Much more slowly than any airplanes I have ever seen. It was weird.

Then suddenly, I saw more lights behind me, all different colors. So I stopped the car and got out. It was like a fireworks display—red, blue, green, and then these white lights in a circle around me. And it was very quiet. I stood there holding on to the car, waiting to see what would happen next. I wasn't scared. I just felt kind of fascinated. It must have gone on for perhaps an hour. Then suddenly, it all disappeared, and I was in the dark.

What did I do next? Well, I sat in my car for a while, because the bright lights had made my eyes a bit funny. And I tried to calm down. In my mind, I was trying to find a rational explanation for it. But to tell you the truth, to this day, I have no idea what it was.

3. Have students write the answers in the chart.

4. Play or read the story again for students to check their answers.

5. Ask volunteers for their answers.

> **Answers:**
> 1. four years ago in the summer, about eight in the evening
> 2. driving home from work
> 3. a string of bright lights in the sky and different colored lights behind him
> 4. he stopped the car and got out
> 5. for about an hour
> 6. fascinated
> 7. sat in his car and tried to calm down
> 8. he has no explanation for it
> Headline: *Answers will vary*

## Give It a Try

### Part 1

1. Have students read the directions and look at the pictures and the categories.

2. Group Work. Divide the class into groups of three or four. Give students time to individually write three sports under each adjective. Have students share their individual lists with their group and give their reasons for putting each sport under each adjective.

### Part 2

1. Have students read the directions.

2. Group Work. Have students discuss if they have done any of the sports listed and what their experience was.

3. Have groups report their discussion to the class.

## Listen To This Unit 12

**Class CD 2, Track 68**

### Part 1

1. Have students read the directions and look at the chart.

2. Play or read the discussion.

M: The question of censorship on the Internet always raises a lot of controversy. Tonight we'll hear opinions from people from four different countries. Our guests tonight are Roger from Canada, Tomomi from Japan, Antonio from Italy, and Frank from Hong Kong. Roger, let's start with you.

R: I'm against any sort of government censorship on the Internet. I think the Internet should be freely available to everyone who wants to express his or her opinion. Once you start trying to control it, it just becomes a political tool for the government.

T: I disagree with Roger. I think that there are a lot of harmful sites on the Web that are not suitable for children. I think it's fine if parents or schools want to control what children can access on the Internet.

M: That's a good point. So you think censorship is OK. Antonio, what do you think?

A: I think Tomomi is right. We do need some kind of censorship to make sure that the Internet is educational and not used for criminal purposes.

M: Frank, what's your opinion?

F: Well, I know it sounds strange, but I think that children have to learn to distinguish good and bad on the Internet, just as they do in real life. We can't protect them all the time. They have to learn to protect themselves. So I guess I am against any kind of censorship.

M: Thank you, guests. You've heard some opinions from around the world. Now we want to hear your opinions. E-mail us with your comments at www.news.com.

3. Have students fill in the chart.

4. Play or read the discussion again for students to check their answers.

5. Ask volunteers for their answers.

| **Answers:** |
| --- |
| Roger: against; doesn't want it to become political tool for the government |
| Tomomi: for; but only for parents and schools controlling what children access on the Internet |
| Antonio: for; Internet should be used for educational and not criminal purposes |
| Frank: against; children need to learn to distinguish good and bad and protect themselves, is against any kind of censorship |

### Part 2

1. Have students read the directions.

2. Group Work. Divide the class into groups. Have groups discuss other reasons for or against censorship of the Internet.

3. Class Work. Have groups report their discussion to the class and continue the discussion.

## Give It a Try

1. Have students read the directions.

2. Group Work. Have students take turns describing a well-known book or movie to the group. Have the rest of the group guess which book or movie it is.

# Optional Activities Teacher's Notes

## Optional Activity 1.1:

### Blind Date, *page 113*

**Preparation:** Copy Optional Activity 1.1 and separate the six role cards. Prepare one role card for each student. Students use the information on their card to have conversations with the other characters in their group, and try to identify who would be the best date for their persona.

**Procedure:** Arrange students into groups of 6 and distribute the role cards. Students review the information on their cards and prepare to have conversations with each persona in their group. After 8-10 minutes of mingling ask the groups to discuss and decide which personas are the best matches.

**Note:** Men can role-play girls and girls can role-play men if necessary.

**Answers:** There are no correct answers for this activity but suggested couples are:

Kumi & Takahiro (hobbies and vacations)
Hikaru & Jie (sports and vacations)
Hirono & Seok Woo (studies, hobbies, and vacations)

## Optional Activity 1.2:

### How well do you know me? *page 114*

**Preparation:** Make one copy of Optional Activity 1.2 for each student.

**Procedure:** Arrange students into pairs. Distribute the handout to each student. Ask students to complete the sentence stems as if they are their partner. They should not communicate with their partner while they are doing this. When everyone is finished, ask partners to share their ideas together.

**Answers:** This is an open, humanistic activity designed to help students relax and get to know each other.

## Optional Activity 2.1:

### My Town, *page 115*

**Preparation:** Make one copy of Optional Activity 2.1 for each student.

**Procedure:** Arrange students into pairs. Distribute the handout and ask students to read the clues to each other and identify the street names.

**Answers:**

A. 1st Avenue
B. 2nd Avenue
C. 3rd Avenue
D. 4th Avenue
E. 5th Avenue
F. Knight Lane
G. Times Boulevard
H. Queen Street

**Additional dialogue practice:** Students add buildings and services to the map and then give directions to a new partner who uses the oral information to draw the new item onto their map.

## Optional Activity 2.2:

### Finding Things in Common, *page 116*

**Preparation:** Make one copy of Optional Activity 2.2 for each student.

**Procedure:** Arrange students into groups of three. Distribute the handout to each student. Ask students to read the words aloud to each other then organize the words into five categories. If students are having trouble finding categories, you could give them one or some of the category labels to get them started. Students may find other categories for the words which is fine if they can defend their choices.

**Suggested Answers:**

1. Places to Shop  bazaar, department store, mall, shopping center, drugstore
2. Construction Materials  glass, stone, brick, concrete, steel
3. Electronics  keyboard, computer, stereo, video games, TV
4. Jewelry  bracelet, watch, ring, necklace, gold chain
5. Clothing  sweater, coat, T-shirt, jeans, shoes

**Additional dialogue practice:** Ask groups to create new categories with five new words in each. Arrange students into new pairs. Each student reads a word set and their partner tries to guess the category to which the words belong.

## Optional Activity 3.1:

### Who's Calling?, *page 117*

**Preparation:** Make one copy of Optional Activity 3.1 for each student.

**Procedure:** Arrange students into pairs. Distribute the handout to each student. Students read through the dialogue and complete them with the appropriate lines from the list.

**Answers:**

Formal   8, 4, 6, 10
Informal  12, 9, 2, 11
Impolite  1, 3, 5, 7

**Additional dialogue practice:** Students role-play the dialogues and exaggerate non-lexical features such as pitch, tone, speed, and intonation.

# Optional Activity 3.2:

## Txt Mssgz, *page 118*

**Preparation:** Make one copy of Optional Activity 3.2 for each student.

**Procedure:** Arrange students into pairs. Distribute the handout to each student. Ask students to use the keypad information to decode the words that appear as numbers in the dialogue.

**Answers:**

A: Hello?
B: Hi Jenny. It's Xi.
A: Hi Xi. What's up?
B: I wrote down those books you wanted but I didn't write down the authors. If I read the names of the books, can you tell me who wrote them?
A: Sure.
B: OK. The first book is called A Long Walk Home.
A: Ah, that was written by Miss D. Bus.
B: Great, and what about Country Living?
A: Let me think. That's by Teresa Greene.
B: Thanks a lot, Jenny. I'll get them to you ASAP.

**Additional dialogue practice:** Students work together to create a new dialogue using the numerical code for some of the key words. Students switch dialogues and decode each others' missing words.

# Optional Activity 4.1:

## New Roommates, *page 119*

**Preparation:** Make one copy of Optional Activity 4.1 for each student.

**Procedure:** Arrange students into pairs. Distribute the handout to each student. Students follow instructions on the handout.

**Answers:** This is an open, personalized discussion. There are no right or wrong ways to do this task as long as the students are giving and defending opinions, and seeking consensus with their partner.

**Additional dialogue practice:** Students work with new groups and take turns presenting their room, and explaining how they reached consensus with their partner.

# Optional Activity 4.2:

## Technology Then and Now, *page 120*

**Preparation:** Make one copy of Optional Activity 4.2 for each student.

**Procedure:** Arrange students into pairs. Distribute the handout to each student. Students discuss items and match old and new technologies from the two lists.

Elicit answers from the class. Students may be unfamiliar with older technologies so be ready to describe them.

In pairs or groups of three, students discuss the personalization questions. Students should aim to use functional language from the unit to identify disadvantages, and explain actions and consequences.

**Answers:**

1. E
2. A
3. G
4. D
5. C
6. B
7. F

**Additional dialogue practice:** Students create and role-play a short scene where a younger person is trying to convince a grandparent to buy or try a new type of technology.

# Optional Activity 5.1:

## Playing Pollyanna, *page 121*

**Preparation:** Make a copy of Optional Activity 5.1 for each student.

**Procedure:** Arrange students into pairs. Distribute the handout to each student. Students read through the Pollyanna text and instructions, then work together to discuss and complete task.

**Suggested Answers:**

1. Kumi won a million dollars. (good)
2. Hank was laid-off from his job.(bad)
3. Jackie went on vacation but caught a virus. (good and bad)
4. Someone stole Christine's laptop computer. (bad)
5. Mei's shoe broke on the way to work. (bad)
6. Noriko's new apartment is only three blocks from the university. (either good or bad)
7. Eva found fifty dollars on the sidewalk.(good)

**Additional dialogue practice:** Students work together and play Pollyanna with new situations.

## Optional Activity 5.2:

### Tongue Twister Whispers, *page 122*

**Preparation:** Teams will write on the classroom board. Each team will need chalk or a marker, and an eraser.

Make a single photocopy of Optional Activity 5.2. You will control the copy and show one tongue twister at a time to the last member of each team. Rolling the bottom edge of the sheet to cover the text is an easy solution.

**Procedure:** 6-8 students stand in single-file teams facing the board.

The instructor stands at the back of the lines, and invites the last student in each line to come forward and read the tongue twister. The students remember as much as possible, return to the back of their line and whisper whatever they can remember to the next student in line. Each student will repeat what they heard to the student in front of them. When the tongue twister arrives to the front, the first student writes it on the board then goes at the back of the line to compare the versions. If what is written on the board is good, the next student in line reads and whispers the next item on the list. The team that "wins" has the most items with the least number of mistakes written on the board when the game ends.

**Note:** The instructor can choose to control this game with a time limit or with a certain number of tongue twisters.

## Optional Activity 6.1:

### Health and Medicine Interview, *page 123*

**Preparation:** Make one copy of Optional Activity 6.1 for each student.

**Procedure:** Arrange students into pairs. Distribute the handout to each student. Students read through the question stems and discuss how to formulate them for the survey.

Elicit some question transformations before the students begin the activity.

*For example:* *…drinks warm water for stomachaches? = Do you drink warm water for stomachaches?*
*…has never been to a dentist = Have you ever been to a dentist?*

Reseat student with a new partner. Students take turns asking their partner questions from the interview sheet. Encourage them to ask each other for additional information which they should note down on their sheets.

Wrap up the activity by eliciting a few responses from students.

**Answers:** This is a personalization activity with no specific answers.

---

**Additional dialogue practice:** Students add additional medical treatment questions to the survey. Be careful about medical conditions as students may be uncomfortable sharing such personal information.

After students have finished interviewing each other, reseat them in small groups and have them discuss the information they discovered about their classmates.

## Optional Activity 6.2:

### Aunt Agony, *page 124*

**Preparation:** Cut Optional Activity 6.2 into three, individual texts, or make one copy of Optional Activity 6.2 for each student. Be prepared to quickly review affirmative and negative modals for giving opinions and advice.

**Procedure:** Arrange students into pairs. Depending on the time limit and linguistic challenge for students, you can distribute just one text to each pair, or distribute the handout with all three texts on it.

Students read the Aunt Agony letter(s) together. They should discuss the possible causes of the problem and try to formulate ways to solve the person's problem.

**Answers:** This is a personalization activity with no specific answers.

**Additional dialogue practice:**

Students create new Aunt Agony letters and exchange them with other pairs.

## Optional Activity 7.1:

### How Many Ways?, *page 125*

**Preparation:** Make a copy of Optional Activity 7.1 for each student. You will need a way to time one-minute intervals.

**Procedure:** Model an item with the class before they start the activity.

*For example:* *You can…rub it on your body, eat it, slide on it, put it in your hair, use it in a burner, fry food in it, float it on water.*

*The answer is OIL.*

Arrange students into pairs. Distribute a handout to each student.

A. Students work together and choose an item from the list of items on the activity sheet.

B. Pairs have one minute to think of and write down as many uses of the item without naming it.

C. Repeat steps A and B for two more items. Every student should now have lists that describe uses for three items.

D. Students work with a new partner(s) and use their list to describe the ways to use an item.

Students may describe or give instructions on how to use the item. They should not say which item they are describing until their partner guesses correctly.

E. Students switch roles and play again with a new item.

**Answers:** This is a personalization activity with no specific answers.

**Variation:** Students can suggest a different set of items or the teacher can select a theme which students can work from. For example, *classroom items, emotions, the environment*, etc.

## Optional Activity 7.2:

### Split Crossword: Travel, *page 126*

**Preparation:** Copy and cut Optional Activity 7.2 into halves.

**Procedure:** This is an information gap activity. Arrange students into pairs. Distribute "Student A" to one student and "Student B" to the other student in each pair. Students must keep their handouts out of their partner's view.

Student A asks for information on a missing word. Student B cannot say the word but instead must give Student A information and clues about the word to help Student A guess. Once Student A has the first word, the students switch roles and Student B asks for information about a missing word. Once all the missing words are complete, students should compare their sheets to confirm the answers and spelling.

**Answers:**

## Optional Activity 8.1:

### Sunny Side Inn Puzzle, *page 127*

**Preparation:** Make a copy of Optional Activity 8.1 for each student.

**Procedure:** Arrange students into pairs. Explain the context of the puzzle. Distribute the handout. Students discuss the clues and complete the chart together. When most of the class is finished, elicit answers and write them on the board.

Strong classes could complete the activity under competition conditions.

**Answers:**

| | |
|---|---|
| Room 101, John and Sally | suite, pool view, Internet access, golf lessons |
| Room 102, Bob and Doug | twin room, golf course view, non-smoking, scuba diving |
| Room 103, Jill and Bill | single room, garden view, cot, tours |
| Room 104, Sue and May | double room, ocean view, limousine service, spa |

**Additional Practice:** Students can role-play guests making reservations by phone or guests arriving and checking-in.

## Optional Activity 8.2:

### Hotel Dialogues, *page 128*

**Preparation:** This is a large group activity. Copy and cut Optional Activity 8.2 into individual strips—10 guest cards and 10 clerk cards.

**Note:** Ensure that for every guest card you distribute that there is a matching clerk card. Participate yourself if there is an odd number of students.

**Procedure:** Tell students that they have Guest cards and Clerk cards, and that they must say their piece of dialogue aloud to find their partner. They may not read each others' cards.

Distribute one card to each student in the class. Ensure that you distrubute matching Guest and Clerk cards among the students.

Students mingle, saying their pieces of dialogue to each other until they find their match. Once they find their match, they should try to continue the dialogue for one or two more turns each.

**Answers:**

Guest: I'd like extra towels in my room, please.
Clerk: I'll send some up right away. How many would you like?
Guest: Hello, I'd like to make a reservation for tonight.
Clerk: Certainly. What size room would you like?

Guest: I'd like a room with an ocean view, please.

Clerk: I'm sorry, they're all taken. I can offer you a room with a garden view.

Guest: Room service? I'd like to order breakfast, please.

Clerk: Certainly. Would you like the breakfast special?

Guest: I need a wake up call for tomorrow morning, please.

Clerk: Of course. What time would you like the call?

Guest: Does your hotel have a fitness center?

Clerk: Yes, we do. We also have an indoor pool.

Guest: How far is your hotel from the beach?

Clerk: The beach is just a short walk through the hotel garden.

Guest: Do you have transportation to and from the airport?

Clerk: Yes, there is a shuttle bus service which stops at our hotel.

Guest: Are any meals included in the price?

Clerk: No, there aren't, but there is a restaurant and coffee shop in the hotel.

Guest: Does your hotel arrange tours of local sights?

Clerk: Yes, the concierge desk can help you book tours.

**Additional dialogue practice:** Pairs can create a short dialogue (4-6 lines) which incorporates the dialogue from their cards and after some practice, role-play them for another pair or the class.

## Optional Activity 9.1:

### Vacation Ranking, *page 129*

**Preparation:** Make a copy of Optional Activity 9.1 for each student.

**Procedure:** In pairs, students read through the list and tell each other what they know about each type of vacation. Individually, students select and rank their six preferred vacations.

Reorganize students into small groups and ask them to compare their selections and discuss their choices with the group.

**Answers:** This is a personalization activity, with no specific answers.

**Additional dialogue practice:** Groups discuss the options and have to agree on one type of vacation that they would all agree to take. Students should also try to agree on where the group would take this vacation, and for how long.

## Optional Activity 9.2:

### Name Three Board Game, *page 130*

**Preparation:** Bring dice and enough counters for each group. Make one copy of Optional Activity 9.2 for each group.

**Procedure:** Arrange students into groups of 4-6. Distribute a handout, a die, and counters to each group. Explain how to play the game to the students.

**How to play the Name Three board game:**

Take turns rolling the die and moving your counter forward.

Read your square aloud to the group and give three answers. Three correct answers give you another throw.

Players cannot repeat answers previously given. If they do, they automatically miss a turn.

Miss a Turn means you cannot progress on this turn.

Free Turn means you do not have to answer correctly to throw again.

The winner is the first player to land on the final clue and answer it correctly.

Explain that each group is responsible for deciding if answers are acceptable but that you will mediate any disagreements.

**Additional dialogue practice:** Students create new categories and reuse the board game structure and rules.

## Optional Activity 10.1:

### Find Someone Who..., *page 131*

**Preparation:** Make a copy of Optional Activity 10.1 for each student.

**Procedure:** Arrange students into pairs. Distribute the handout to each student. Students read through the sentence stems together and discuss how to ask each question.

Elicit some question transformations before the students begin the activity.

*For example: ...is someone's grandchild. = Are you someone's grandchild?*
*...has never been aboard a boat. = Have you ever been aboard a boat? (Note: Students need to look for a "NO" answer.)*

As a whole class or in large groups, students interview individual classmates until they find someone who can say the information is true for them. Students then write that person's name on the sheet, and then interview the person to get more information about their answer.

Encourage students to interview as many people as possible and to note down as many details as they can.

**Answers:** This is a personalization activity with no specific answers.

## Optional Activity 10.2:

### What's My Role?, *page 132*

**Preparation:** Make copies of Optional Activity 10.2 and cut the sheet into individual roles. Prepare a set of role cards for each group.

Arrange students into groups of 4-5. Place the role cards face down on the table between players.

**Note:** It is important that students do not see the roles before the game begins. Role cards should not be returned to the pile.

**Procedure:** A student volunteers to be the first player. Another student takes a role card from the top of the pile and shows it to everyone in the group except the volunteer. The group has 90 seconds to help the volunteer guess the role on the card. The members of the group should spontaneously give hints and clues about the characteristics of the role on the card. They should not say what the role is or give very obvious clues. The volunteer can ask Yes/No questions. Information questions are not allowed. The volunteer may try to guess the role at any time. However, the time limit is only 90 seconds for each role. When time is up, another student volunteers to play and the game continues until all students have had an opportunity to guess a role.

**Answers:** This is an open, collaborative activity with no specific answers.

**Further practice:** Students work in pairs or small groups to role-play job interviews. One student is interviewed for the role on their card. They should explain why they would be the best candidate for this role.

## Optional Activity 11.1:

### Food Survey, *page 133*

**Preparation:** Make a copy of Optional Activity 11.1 for each student.

**Procedure:** Distribute the handout to each student. Students read through the items on the survey and add two more items. Indvidually, students complete the survey with their own information. In the case that students have not tried any of the items on the list, ask them to list the most exotic food/drinks they have tried.

In pairs, students interview each other regarding the cues and then discuss their experiences and opinions.

**Answers:** This is an interview activity with no specific answers.

## Optional Activity 11.2:

### On the Spot Stories, *page 134*

**Preparation:** Make a copy of Optional Activity 11.2 for each group. Cut the material into "How to" instructions, and sets of event cards cut into individual strips.

**Procedure:** Arrange students into groups of 4-6 students. Distribute the "How to" instructions and a set of event cards to each group. Ask students to put the event cards face down on the table.

A student picks up an event card.

The student reads the event card to begin an interesting story.

The group asks questions about the story using question forms found in the unit, and the student answers immediately, making up the story on-the-spot.

Each story is finished after eight questions and answers, or after three minutes of questions and answers.

Another student picks up an Event Card, and a new story begins.

**Answers:** This is an interview/role-play activity with no specific answers.

**Variations:** Give one event card to each group. Students work together to create a story from their event card. Reseat the students into new groups where each student has a different story. Students share their stories and answer new questions from the group.

## Optional Activity 12.1:

### Fast-food Reviews, *page 135*

**Preparation:** Make a copy of Optional Activity 12.1 for each student.

**Procedure:** Arrange students into small groups (3-4 students). Distribute a handout to each student. Students work together to complete the tasks on the handout.

The review stage of the activity could be made more formal, with students presenting to larger groups, and in more detail. A teacher-centered discussion could also be held at the end of the activity to discuss the information presented during the reviews. Did the reviews change anyone's opinion about fast food restaurants?

**Answers:** This is a discussion and opinion activity with no specific answers.

### Battle of the Sexes, *page 136*

**Preparation:** Make a copy of Optional Activity 12.2 for each student.

**Procedure:** Distribute the handout to each student. Individually, students read through the statements and rate them on a 1–4 scale. Arrange students into small groups. Attempt to arrange groups so there are both men and women in each group. Ask groups to discuss their reactions to each of the statements. Encourage students to be polite, but to defend their opinions.

**Answers:** This is a personalized discussion which promotes opinions rather than answers.

**Additional dialogue practice:** Students discuss and write down other gender specific stereotypes they are aware of. Further discussion could be teacher-centered or students could be rearranged into small groups to discuss the students' ideas.

**Teacher:**  Cut the sheet into individual roles.

✂ - - - - - - - - - - - - - - - - - - - - - - - - - - - - -

|  | Name:  Kumi |
|---|---|
| Job | Where:  none |
|  | What:  none |
| Studies | Where:  a state university |
|  | What:  Business |
|  | Hobbies:  Reading mystery novels |
|  | Sports:  Tennis |
|  | Musical taste:  Classical |
| Last Vacation | When:  Last summer |
|  | Where:  Australia |

✂ - - - - - - - - - - - - - - - - - - - - - - - - - - - - -

|  | Name:  Jie |
|---|---|
| Job | Where:  none |
|  | What:  none |
| Studies | Where:  a private university |
|  | What:  Medicine |
|  | Hobbies:  Singing |
|  | Sports:  Basketball |
|  | Musical taste:  All types of music |
| Last Vacation | When:  Four years ago |
|  | Where:  Stayed home |

✂ - - - - - - - - - - - - - - - - - - - - - - - - - - - - -

|  | Name:  Hikaru |
|---|---|
| Job | Where:  a department store |
|  | What:  greeter |
| Studies | Where:  a school for performing arts |
|  | What:  Modern dance |
|  | Hobbies:  Designing dance costumes |
|  | Sports:  Basketball |
|  | Musical taste:  Rap music |
| Last Vacation | When:  Three years ago |
|  | Where: Stayed home |

✂ - - - - - - - - - - - - - - - - - - - - - - - - - - - - -

|  | Name:  Seok Woo |
|---|---|
| Job | Where:  none |
|  | What:  none |
| Studies | Where:  an art college |
|  | What:  Fashion Design |
|  | Hobbies:  Drawing pictures |
|  | Sports:  Soccer |
|  | Musical taste:  Hip Hop |
| Last Vacation | When:  Can't remember. |
|  | Where:  Can't remember. |

✂ - - - - - - - - - - - - - - - - - - - - - - - - - - - - -

|  | Name:  Hirono |
|---|---|
| Job | Where:  none |
|  | What:  none |
| Studies | Where:  an art college |
|  | What:  Film |
|  | Hobbies:  Painting |
|  | Sports:  Tennis |
|  | Musical taste:  Rock |
| Last Vacation | When:  Can't remember. |
|  | Where:  Can't remember. |

✂ - - - - - - - - - - - - - - - - - - - - - - - - - - - - -

|  | Name:  Takahiro |
|---|---|
| Job | Where:  a movie theater |
|  | What:  part-time cashier |
| Studies | Where:  a state music school |
|  | What:  Violin |
|  | Hobbies:  Reading mystery novels |
|  | Sports:  Baseball |
|  | Musical taste:  Classical |
| Last Vacation | When:  Last summer |
|  | Where:  New Zealand and Australia |

## Optional Activity 1.2: How well do you know me?

*Part 1*  Read the statements. Imagine you are your partner. Complete the statements like you think your partner would. Do not communicate with your partner until your teacher tells you to.

1.  On the weekends I always _____ .

2.  I show my creativity by _____ .

3.  I mostly use my computer to _____ .

4.  The most important thing in my life is _____ .

5.  Every day I _____ .

6.  In my spare time I like to _____ .

7.  My favorite time of day is _____ .

8.  I have never _____ .

9.  On my birthday I always _____ .

10. The best room in my house is _____ .

*Part 2*  Share your guesses with your partner. Were you right? Discuss why you both made the choices you did. Does anything surprise you?

Work with a partner. Use the clues below to name the streets (A–H) on the map.
Write your answers below.

1. From City Park, cross Third Avenue to visit the Queen Street shopping center.

2. Queen Street ends at the intersection of Third Avenue and Oceanside Road.

3. The United Office Tower is on the corner of Knight Lane and Third Avenue.

4. There are two downtown subway stations. One is on the corner of Second Avenue and Queen Street.

5. The Midnight Cafe faces First Avenue which is also the city's freeway.

6. Visit the historic Capital Clock Tower on Times Boulevard.

7. The Fourth Avenue subway station is right across from the City Park, on the corner of Times Boulevard and Fourth Avenue.

8. Hire a bike on Fifth Avenue, just a block from the Central High School.

A. _____    B. _____    C. _____    D. _____

E. _____    F. _____    G. _____    H. _____

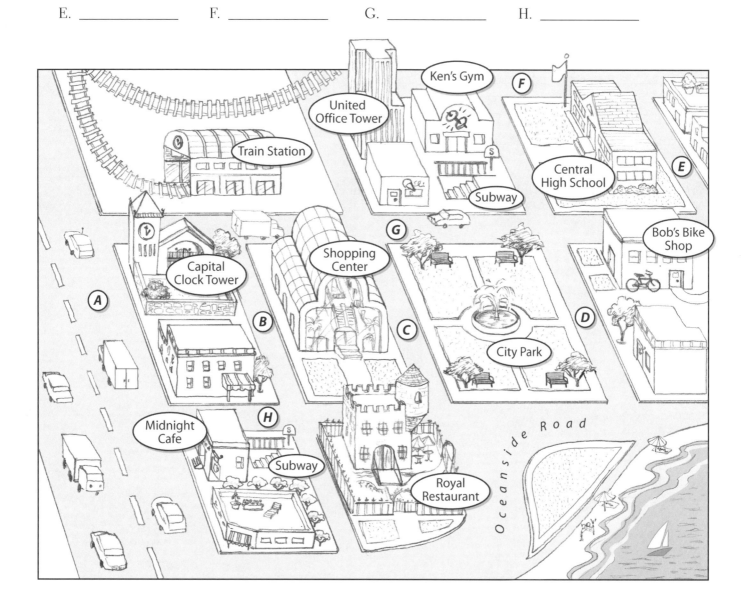

*Part 1*   Work in groups of three. Read through the words in the list. Organize the words into five categories. Label each category. You can use items more than once.

| | | | | |
|---|---|---|---|---|
| sweater | bazaar | gold chain | glass | ring |
| department store | stone | coat | necklace | brick |
| keyboard | T-shirt | computer | shopping center | jeans |
| watch | stereo | concrete | bracelet | mall |
| video games | shoes | steel | drugstore | TV |

1. _____   2. _____   3. _____   4. _____   5. _____

_____   _____   _____   _____   _____

_____   _____   _____   _____   _____

_____   _____   _____   _____   _____

_____   _____   _____   _____   _____

_____   _____   _____   _____   _____

_____   _____   _____   _____   _____

_____   _____   _____   _____   _____

_____   _____   _____   _____   _____

*Part 2*   Add three more words to each category. Compare your categories and word lists with a new partner.

Work with a partner. Complete the phone conversations with the lines below.

1. I want to speak to Lam.
2. OK. I'll get her.
3. Oh, when will he be home?
4. Yes, thank you. My name's Akira and I play in the band.
5. Tonight?
6. I don't think so. This was my first week in the band.
7. I have no idea.
8. Hello. Could I speak to Hiro, please?
9. It's Gemma. We go to class together.
10. Yes, he does. Thank you.
11. No problem.
12. Sure. Who's calling?

## Formal

A: _____ .

B: I'm sorry, he's not here.  Can I take a message?

A: _____ .

B: Oh, do you? Have we met?

A: _____ .

B: Well, I'll tell Hiro you called. Does he have your number?

A: _____ .

B: Goodbye.

## Informal

A: Hi, is Yue there, please?

B: _____ .

A: _____ .

B: _____ .

A: Thanks

B: _____ .

## Impolite

A: _____ .

B: He's not here.

A: _____ .

B: I don't know.

A: _____ .

B: _____ .

A: Oh, ok.

Work with a partner. Use the telephone keypad below to break the code and reveal the conversation.

**A:** Hello?

**B:** Hi Jenny. It's Xi.

**A:** __ __ __ __. What's up?
$\quad$ 4 4 9 4

**B:** I __ __ __ __ __ down those __ __ __ __ __ you wanted but I __ __ __ __'__ write down
$\quad\quad$ 9 7 6 8 3 $\quad\quad\quad\quad$ 2 6 6 5 7 $\quad\quad\quad\quad$ 3 4 3 6 8

the __ __ __ __ __ __ __.
$\quad\quad$ 2 8 8 4 6 7 7

$\quad$ __ __ I read the __ __ __ __ __ of the books, __ __ __ you __ __ __ __ me __ __ __
$\quad\quad$ 4 3 $\quad\quad\quad\quad$ 6 2 6 3 7 $\quad\quad\quad\quad$ 2 2 6 $\quad\quad$ 8 3 5 5 $\quad\quad$ 9 4 6

$\quad$ __ __ __ __ __ them?
$\quad\quad$ 9 7 6 8 3

**A:** Sure.

**B:** OK. The __ __ __ __ __ __ book is __ __ __ __ __ __ __ A __ __ __ __ Walk Home.
$\quad\quad\quad\quad$ 3 4 7 7 8 $\quad\quad\quad\quad$ 2 2 5 5 3 3 $\quad\quad$ 5 6 6 4

**A:** Ah, that was __ __ __ __ __ __ __ by Miss D. __ __ __.
$\quad\quad\quad\quad$ 9 7 4 8 8 3 6 $\quad\quad\quad\quad$ 2 8 7

**B:** Great, and what about __ __ __ __ __ __ __ Living?
$\quad\quad\quad\quad$ 2 6 8 6 8 7 9

**A:** Let me __ __ __ __ __. That's __ __ Teresa Greene.
$\quad\quad\quad$ 8 4 4 6 5 $\quad\quad\quad$ 2 9

**B:** Thanks a __ __ __, Jenny. I'll get __ __ __ __ to you __ __ __ __.
$\quad\quad\quad\quad$ 5 6 8 $\quad\quad\quad\quad$ 8 4 3 6 $\quad\quad\quad$ 2 7 2 7

*Part 1*  Imagine you are going to share a dorm room with someone for the next twelve months. List six pieces of furniture that you would take with you. Draw the items here.

*Part 2*  Work with a partner. Compare your furniture lists. Use the floor plan below to agree on how you will share the space in the room. What furniture will fit and what furniture will you have to leave behind? Can you agree on how to arrange the furniture in the room so that you will both be comfortable and happy roommates?

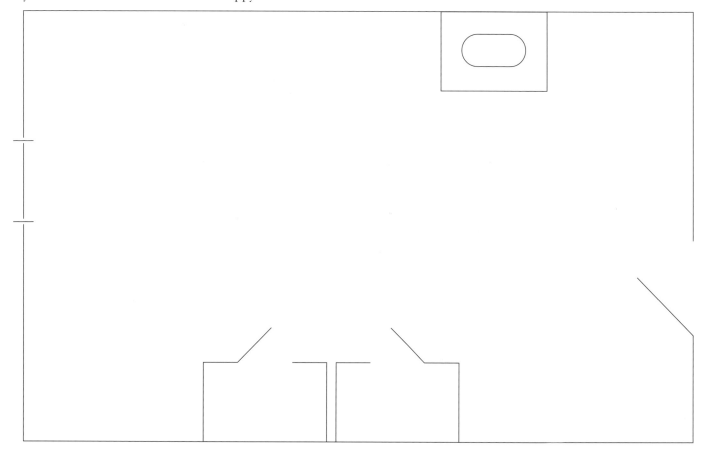

## Optional Activity 4.2: Technology Then and Now

Work with a partner. Match an item from today with an item from the past.

1. MP3 player ____          A. VCR

2. DVD player ____          B. arcade game

3. internet dating ____     C. fax machine

4. voice mail ____          D. answering machine

5. e-mail ____              E. hi-fi stereo system

6. TV games ____            F. electronic typewriter

7. laptop computer ____     G. night club

Which of the items in the lists do you use?
Which of the items do your parents use?
What are the advantages and disadvantages of each item?
How would you convince your grandmother to buy a laptop computer?

Pollyanna was the young heroine of a famous American novel. She became famous because she always tried to see the bright side of every situation, even very difficult ones.

Work with a partner. Read the following situations and decide if they are good news or bad news. If they are bad news, then imagine you are Pollyanna and think of three positive ways to see the situation. For example: *Peter broke his leg.* (This is bad news.)

Three good things about it are:

1. He doesn't have to go to work for a few days.
2. He has time to surf the web.
3. Everyone will be extra nice to him until he gets better.

If the situation is good news, try to think of three negative things to say about the situation.

1. Kumi won a million dollars.
2. Hank was laid-off from his job.
3. Jackie went on vacation, but caught the flu.
4. Someone stole Christine's laptop computer.
5. Mei's shoe broke on the way to work.
6. Noriko's new apartment is only three blocks from the university.
7. Eva found $50 on the sidewalk.

**Teacher:**  Show tongue twisters one at a time. Roll the bottom edge of the sheet to cover the text
so that students can only read the current tongue twister.

---

Around the rugged rocks the ragged rat ran.

---

Suzie's shop stocks boxes of short spotted socks.

---

Big blue bugs bleed bright blue blood.

---

Mrs. Smith owns a fish sauce shop.

---

Robbie ran rings around the remaining Roman ruins.

---

Three gray geese in the green grass grazing.

---

Elizabeth's birthday is on the third Thursday of the month.

---

Lesser leather never weathered wetter weather better.

---

*Part 1*  In pairs, read through the cues on the survey sheet. Discuss and agree on how to ask the questions. Be careful of the negative statements on the list!

*Part 2*  Work with a new partner. Use questions on the interview sheet to interview your classmate. Write down as many details as possible about your classmate.

**Classmate:** _____

| | |
|---|---|
| ever had acupuncture? | |
| take aspirin for headaches? | |
| get plenty of regular exercise? | |
| never missed a day of school due to bad health? | |
| know how to meditate? | |
| take herbs for stomachaches? | |
| ever had a tooth pulled? | |
| have a gym membership? | |
| can give massages? | |
| never been x-rayed? | |
| had a broken arm? | |
| regularly visit a doctor for a complete check-up? | |
| sleep eight hours a night? | |

Work with a partner. Read the letters. Discuss the advice you would give to solve each person's problem.

*Dear Aunt Agony,*

*I started my first full time job a couple of months ago. I am enjoying the work but some of the people in the office are a little noisy. There are no walls in our office, and there is this guy who sits about five desks away. He has his radio on all the time and won't turn it down. Then there is this other woman who speaks so loudly on the phone. She is always talking to her friends and her boyfriend. I have asked other people in the office for advice, but they all say there is nothing that can be done. What can I do to have a quieter place to work?*

*Quiet Wanted*

Dear Aunt Agony,

I have a serious problem. My new roommate is really messy. I didn't know that he was this way until he arrived in the summer. I tried to be polite, picked things up, and tried to ignore it. But now it's been six months and he is getting even messier. He almost never washes the dishes or his clothes. My friends refuse to visit me. I don't want a new roommate but something has to change. What should I do?

Neat Guy

Dear Aunt Agony,

How can I stop being so lazy? I just can't find a way to get motivated. I finished my final exams last month and since then I just seem to sleep all the time. I never seem to get anything done, and my friends have stopped calling because I never want to leave the house. I still live with my parents so I don't have to worry about paying bills, but I am scared that I will lose my friends, and that my parents will throw me out if I don't start doing things soon. How can I stop being so tired, and turn my life around?

Unmotivated

**Part 1** Work with a partner. Together, choose an item from the list below. In one minute, think of as many ways to use the item as possible. Write down your ideas. Repeat steps A and B for two more items. Now you have lists of ways to use three items.

**Part 2** Work with a new partner. Do not say which item you are describing until your partner guesses correctly. List your uses for the item. Start with the most unusual. When your partner guesses the item, switch roles, and play again with a new item.

# Optional Activity 7.2: Split Crossword: Travel

## Student A

Useful Expressions

| Questions | Answers |
| --- | --- |
| Why do I need number three across? | You need it to/for… |
| What is number three across used for? | If you don't have it/them, you… |

Crossword grid (Student A) — visible letters:

- 1 down: B O O K
- 2 down: J O U R N A L
- 3 across: E … (EMERGENCY …)
- 4 down: E M E R G E N C Y N U M B E R S
- 5 down: P H O N E
- 6 down: P A S S P O R T
- 9 down: S U N S C R E E N
- 10 down: M O N E Y B E L T
- 14 down: M A P S
- 7 across, 8 across, 11 across, 12 across, 13 across (T…), 15 across (S…), 16 across (S…)

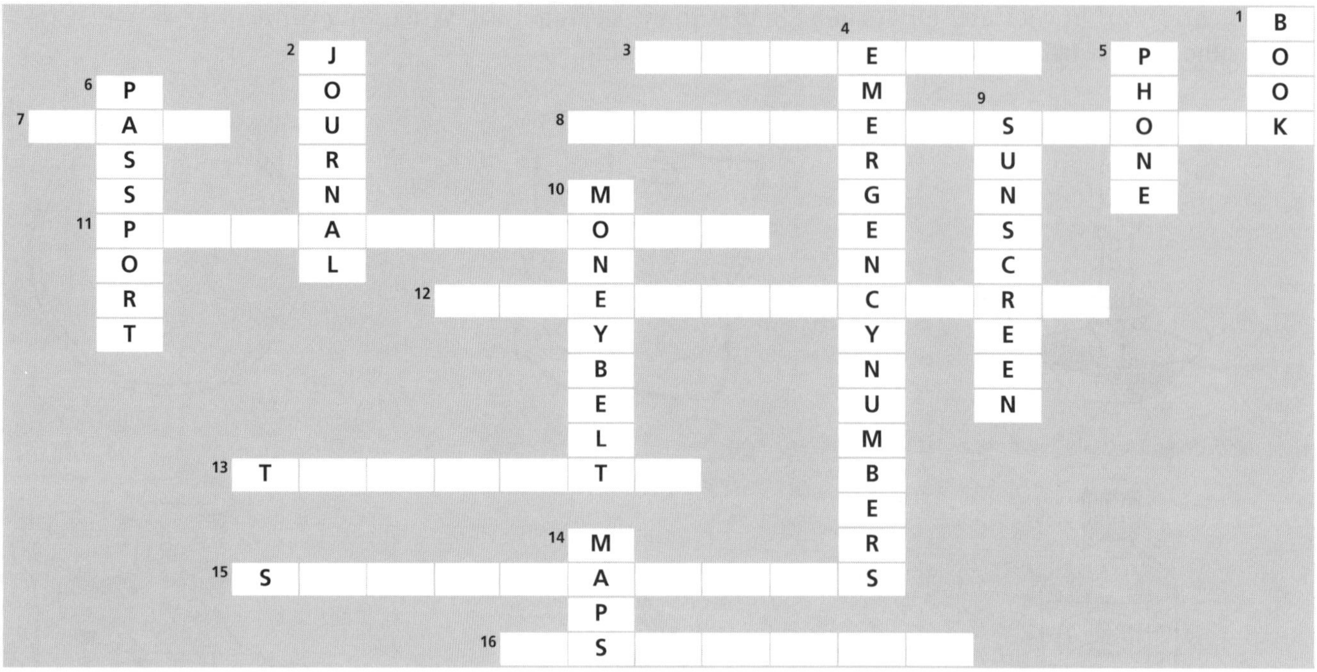

## Student B

Useful Expressions

| Questions | Answers |
| --- | --- |
| Why do I need number one down? | You need it to/for… |
| What is number one down used for? | If you don't have it/them, you… |

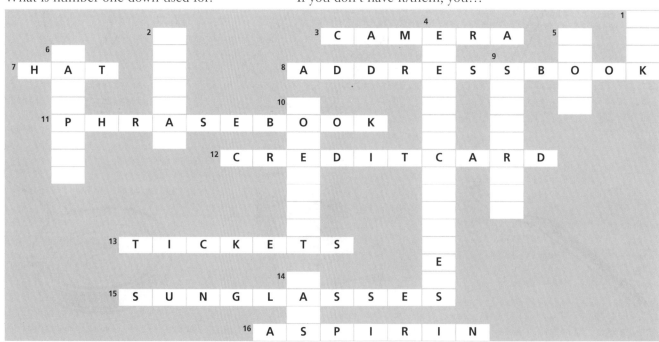

Crossword grid (Student B) — visible letters:

- 3 across: C A M E R A
- 7 across: H A T
- 8 across: A D D R E S S B O O K
- 11 across: P H R A S E B O O K
- 12 across: C R E D I T C A R D
- 13 across: T I C K E T S
- 15 across: S U N G L A S S E S
- 16 across: A S P I R I N

The computer system at the Sunny Side Inn crashed and all of the information about the guest reservations was lost. The night clerk remembered a lot of information, but couldn't organize it.

Work with a partner. Discuss the information together and complete the hotel guest chart.

**Hotel Guest Information**

- Bob and Doug are in room 102, and are not next to the room with an ocean view.
- The guests in the single room are between the non-smoking room and the room with the ocean view.
- The room with the pool view belongs to John and Sally, and is not next to the single room.
- Sue and May, who requested the limousine service, are next to the single room.
- Jill and Bill are interested in tours.
- Jill, who requested a cot for her son Bill, is next to the room with a view of the golf course
- The guests interested in scuba diving are between the room with the view of the pool and the room with the view of the garden.
- John and Sally, who are interested in golf lessons, are next to the twin room.
- The guests who requested Internet access are in the suite which is next to the twin room.
- The guests in the double room are interested in the spa facilities.

| Room number | 101 | 102 | 103 | 104 |
|---|---|---|---|---|
| Guests' names | | | | |
| Room size | | | | |
| View from room | | | | |
| Special request | | | | |
| Interest | | | | |

**Teacher:** Cut the sheet into individual strips.

✂ -----------------------------------------------------------------

**Guest:** I'd like extra towels in my room, please.

✂ -----------------------------------------------------------------

**Guest:** Hello, I'd like to make a reservation for tonight.

✂ -----------------------------------------------------------------

**Guest:** I'd like a room with an ocean view, please.

✂ -----------------------------------------------------------------

**Guest:** Room service? I'd like to order breakfast, please.

✂ -----------------------------------------------------------------

**Guest:** I need a wake up call for tomorrow morning, please.

✂ -----------------------------------------------------------------

**Guest:** Does your hotel have a fitness center?

✂ -----------------------------------------------------------------

**Guest:** How far is your hotel from the beach?

✂ -----------------------------------------------------------------

**Guest:** Do you have transportation to and from the airport?

✂ -----------------------------------------------------------------

**Guest:** Are any meals included in the price?

✂ -----------------------------------------------------------------

**Guest:** Does your hotel arrange tours of local sights?

✂ -----------------------------------------------------------------

**Clerk:** I'll send some up right away. How many would you like?

✂ -----------------------------------------------------------------

**Clerk:** Certainly. What size room would you like?

✂ -----------------------------------------------------------------

**Clerk:** I'm sorry, they're all taken. I can offer you a room with a garden view.

✂ -----------------------------------------------------------------

**Clerk:** Certainly. Would you like the breakfast special?

✂ -----------------------------------------------------------------

**Clerk:** Of course. What time would you like the call?

✂ -----------------------------------------------------------------

**Clerk:** Yes, we do. We also have an indoor pool.

✂ -----------------------------------------------------------------

**Clerk:** The beach is just a short walk through the hotel garden.

✂ -----------------------------------------------------------------

**Clerk:** Yes, there is a shuttle bus service which stops at our hotel.

✂ -----------------------------------------------------------------

**Clerk:** No, there aren't, but there is a restaurant and coffee shop in the hotel.

✂ -----------------------------------------------------------------

**Clerk:** Yes, the concierge desk can help you book tours.

✂ -----------------------------------------------------------------

*Part 1*   Work with a partner. Read through the list below. Have you ever taken vacations like these? Individually, choose the six vacations that most interest you. Rank your choices from 1-6. Be ready to explain why you chose these vacations, and how you ranked them.

_____ Beach resort

_____ Mountain climbing

_____ Backpacking

_____ Cruise

_____ African safari

_____ Cultural tour

_____ Educational exchange

_____ Cycling tour

_____ Fitness camp

_____ Surfing and water sports

_____ Skiing

_____ Bus tour

_____ Sailing

_____ Camping

_____ Train trip

_____ Health spa and resort

*Part 2*   Work in small groups. Compare your selection with the group. Discuss your choices.

1. What makes these vacations interesting for you?

2. How far would you travel for these vacations? Where specifically would you go?

3. How long would the vacations be?

How to play:

- Take turns rolling the die and moving your counter forward.

- Read your square aloud to the group and give three answers. Three correct answers give you another throw.

- Players cannot repeat answers previously given. If they do, they automatically miss a turn.

- Miss a Turn means you cannot progress on this turn.

- Free Turn means you do not have to answer correctly to throw again.

- The winner is the first player to land on the final clue and answer it successfully.

To play this game, you need 4-6 players, a die, and a counter for each player.

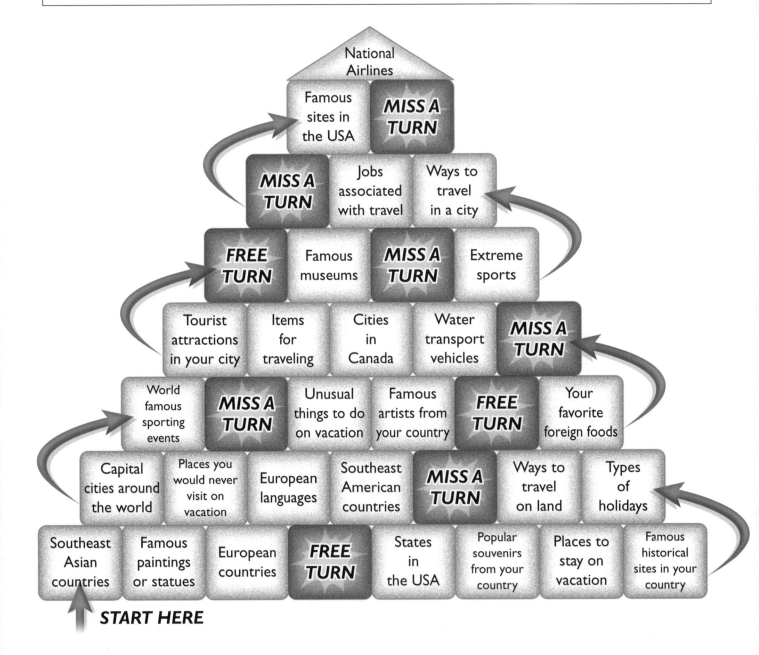

*Part 1*   With a partner, read through the cues below. Discuss and agree on how to ask the questions.
Be careful of the negative statements in the list!

*Part 2*   Interview individual classmates until you find someone who the information is true for.
Write that person's name below, then interview him/her to get more information about his/her
answer. Try to get as many names and additional details on your sheet as possible.

| **Find someone who...** | | |
| --- | --- | --- |
| Name | | Details |
| _____ | has a family pet. | _____ |
| _____ | has more than two siblings (brothers and sisters). | _____ |
| _____ | wants to work in the medical field. | _____ |
| _____ | has traveled to North America. | _____ |
| _____ | is someone's aunt/uncle. | _____ |
| _____ | plays a competitive sport. | _____ |
| _____ | likes to travel by train. | _____ |
| _____ | is the oldest child in his/her family. | _____ |
| _____ | has never traveled outside the country. | _____ |
| _____ | owns a car. | _____ |
| _____ | can play an acoustic guitar. | _____ |
| _____ | has never been in an airplane. | _____ |

**Teacher:** Cut the sheet into individual roles. Prepare one set of roles for each group.

✂ - - - - - - - - - - - - - - - - - - - - - - - - - - - - - - - - - - - - - - - - - - - - - - - - - - - -

university professor

✂ - - - - - - - - - - - - - - - - - - - - - - - - - - - - - - - - - - - - - - - - - - - - - - - - - - - -

chief executive officer

✂ - - - - - - - - - - - - - - - - - - - - - - - - - - - - - - - - - - - - - - - - - - - - - - - - - - - -

teacher

✂ - - - - - - - - - - - - - - - - - - - - - - - - - - - - - - - - - - - - - - - - - - - - - - - - - - - -

surgeon

✂ - - - - - - - - - - - - - - - - - - - - - - - - - - - - - - - - - - - - - - - - - - - - - - - - - - - -

sailor

✂ - - - - - - - - - - - - - - - - - - - - - - - - - - - - - - - - - - - - - - - - - - - - - - - - - - - -

grandparent

✂ - - - - - - - - - - - - - - - - - - - - - - - - - - - - - - - - - - - - - - - - - - - - - - - - - - - -

parent

✂ - - - - - - - - - - - - - - - - - - - - - - - - - - - - - - - - - - - - - - - - - - - - - - - - - - - -

fashion designer

✂ - - - - - - - - - - - - - - - - - - - - - - - - - - - - - - - - - - - - - - - - - - - - - - - - - - - -

older sibling

✂ - - - - - - - - - - - - - - - - - - - - - - - - - - - - - - - - - - - - - - - - - - - - - - - - - - - -

sales representative

✂ - - - - - - - - - - - - - - - - - - - - - - - - - - - - - - - - - - - - - - - - - - - - - - - - - - - -

accountant

✂ - - - - - - - - - - - - - - - - - - - - - - - - - - - - - - - - - - - - - - - - - - - - - - - - - - - -

babysitter

✂ - - - - - - - - - - - - - - - - - - - - - - - - - - - - - - - - - - - - - - - - - - - - - - - - - - - -

hairdresser

✂ - - - - - - - - - - - - - - - - - - - - - - - - - - - - - - - - - - - - - - - - - - - - - - - - - - - -

best friend

✂ - - - - - - - - - - - - - - - - - - - - - - - - - - - - - - - - - - - - - - - - - - - - - - - - - - - -

leader of a nation

✂ - - - - - - - - - - - - - - - - - - - - - - - - - - - - - - - - - - - - - - - - - - - - - - - - - - - -

actor

✂ - - - - - - - - - - - - - - - - - - - - - - - - - - - - - - - - - - - - - - - - - - - - - - - - - - - -

fashion model

✂ - - - - - - - - - - - - - - - - - - - - - - - - - - - - - - - - - - - - - - - - - - - - - - - - - - - -

astronaut

✂ - - - - - - - - - - - - - - - - - - - - - - - - - - - - - - - - - - - - - - - - - - - - - - - - - - - -

good child

✂ - - - - - - - - - - - - - - - - - - - - - - - - - - - - - - - - - - - - - - - - - - - - - - - - - - - -

businessman

✂ - - - - - - - - - - - - - - - - - - - - - - - - - - - - - - - - - - - - - - - - - - - - - - - - - - - -

architect

✂ - - - - - - - - - - - - - - - - - - - - - - - - - - - - - - - - - - - - - - - - - - - - - - - - - - - -

airline pilot

✂ - - - - - - - - - - - - - - - - - - - - - - - - - - - - - - - - - - - - - - - - - - - - - - - - - - - -

# Optional Activity 11.1:  Food Survey

*Part 1*   Read the list of unusual foods, and then add some more exotic foods and drinks to the list.

| | Me | | | My Partner | | |
|---|---|---|---|---|---|---|
| | When? | Where? | How was it? | When? | Where? | How was it? |
| snake | | | | | | |
| lobster | | | | | | |
| caviar | | | | | | |
| kangaroo | | | | | | |
| octopus | | | | | | |
| gelato | | | | | | |
| cow's tongue | | | | | | |
| alligator | | | | | | |
| frog's legs | | | | | | |

*Part 2*   Individually, complete the "me" columns with your own information.

*Part 3*   Interview your partner and collect information about him/her.

*Part 4*   Discuss your answers with your partner. Are your experiences similar?
Would you like to try any of these foods? Is there anything you would never eat? Why?

How to play:

- One student picks up an event card.
- The student reads the event card to begin an interesting story.
- The group asks information questions about the story and the student answers immediately, making up the story on-the-spot.
- Each story is finished after eight questions and answers, or after three minutes of questions and answers.
- Another student picks up an event card, and a new story begins.

To play this game you need a group of 4-6 students and a set of event cards, face down on the table.

✂ - - - - - - - - - - - - - - - - - - - - - - - - - - - - - - - - - - - - - - - - - - - - - - - - - - - - - - - - - - - - - - - - - - - - - - - - -

Have I ever told you about the time I met a famous person?

✂ - - - - - - - - - - - - - - - - - - - - - - - - - - - - - - - - - - - - - - - - - - - - - - - - - - - - - - - - - - - - - - - - - - - - - - - - -

Have I ever told you about the time I was on television?

✂ - - - - - - - - - - - - - - - - - - - - - - - - - - - - - - - - - - - - - - - - - - - - - - - - - - - - - - - - - - - - - - - - - - - - - - - - -

Have I ever told you about the time I fell asleep in English class?

✂ - - - - - - - - - - - - - - - - - - - - - - - - - - - - - - - - - - - - - - - - - - - - - - - - - - - - - - - - - - - - - - - - - - - - - - - - -

Have I ever told you about the time I broke my neighbor's window?

✂ - - - - - - - - - - - - - - - - - - - - - - - - - - - - - - - - - - - - - - - - - - - - - - - - - - - - - - - - - - - - - - - - - - - - - - - - -

Have I ever told you about the time I found an insect in my soup?

✂ - - - - - - - - - - - - - - - - - - - - - - - - - - - - - - - - - - - - - - - - - - - - - - - - - - - - - - - - - - - - - - - - - - - - - - - - -

Have I ever told you about the time I saw a UFO?

✂ - - - - - - - - - - - - - - - - - - - - - - - - - - - - - - - - - - - - - - - - - - - - - - - - - - - - - - - - - - - - - - - - - - - - - - - - -

Have I ever told you about the time I broke my nose?

✂ - - - - - - - - - - - - - - - - - - - - - - - - - - - - - - - - - - - - - - - - - - - - - - - - - - - - - - - - - - - - - - - - - - - - - - - - -

Have I ever told you about the time I won a gold medal?

✂ - - - - - - - - - - - - - - - - - - - - - - - - - - - - - - - - - - - - - - - - - - - - - - - - - - - - - - - - - - - - - - - - - - - - - - - - -

Have I ever told you about the time I fainted on the bus?

✂ - - - - - - - - - - - - - - - - - - - - - - - - - - - - - - - - - - - - - - - - - - - - - - - - - - - - - - - - - - - - - - - - - - - - - - - - -

Have I ever told you about the time I found a treasure map?

✂ - - - - - - - - - - - - - - - - - - - - - - - - - - - - - - - - - - - - - - - - - - - - - - - - - - - - - - - - - - - - - - - - - - - - - - - - -

Have I ever told you about the time I won the lottery?

✂ - - - - - - - - - - - - - - - - - - - - - - - - - - - - - - - - - - - - - - - - - - - - - - - - - - - - - - - - - - - - - - - - - - - - - - - - -

Have I ever told you about the time I sang in front of 200 people?

✂ - - - - - - - - - - - - - - - - - - - - - - - - - - - - - - - - - - - - - - - - - - - - - - - - - - - - - - - - - - - - - - - - - - - - - - - - -

*Part 1*   Discuss these questions with your group.

1. Do you like fast food? Explain.

2. When was the last time you ate at a fast-food restaurant?

3. Do you know when American fast food was introduced to your country?

4. Make a list of the most popular fast-food restaurants in your city.

5. Describe the type of food and drinks you can buy at each restaurant on your list.

*Part 2*   Choose the three restaurants your group members are most familiar with, and write them on the chart below.

*Part 3*   Discuss each restaurant in relation to the five specific categories. Give each restaurant an overall rating out of five stars. Note your ideas for each category on the chart.

| Restaurant | Food Quality | Menu Selection | Service | Cost | Cleanliness | Overall Rating ***** |
|---|---|---|---|---|---|---|
|  |  |  |  |  |  |  |
|  |  |  |  |  |  |  |
|  |  |  |  |  |  |  |

*Part 4*   Work together to select and organize information for a short oral review of a restaurant from your chart.

*Part 5*   In new groups take turns giving reviews of fast-food restaurants in your city.

*Part 1*  Read each statement, and rate them on a scale of 1–4 depending on your reactions.

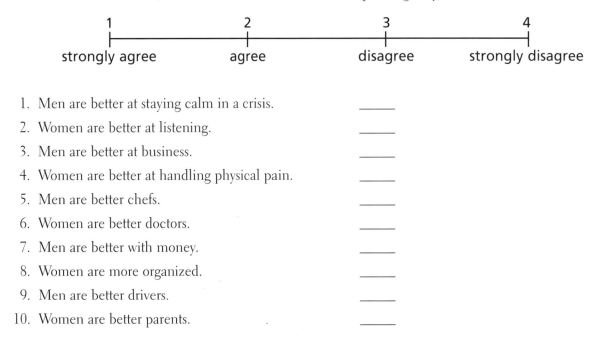

| 1 | 2 | 3 | 4 |
| strongly agree | agree | disagree | strongly disagree |

1. Men are better at staying calm in a crisis.  _____
2. Women are better at listening.  _____
3. Men are better at business.  _____
4. Women are better at handling physical pain.  _____
5. Men are better chefs.  _____
6. Women are better doctors.  _____
7. Men are better with money.  _____
8. Women are more organized.  _____
9. Men are better drivers.  _____
10. Women are better parents.  _____

*Part 2*  In small groups, compare your reactions with the group. Remember to defend your opinions. Don't be afraid to disagree!

Useful Expressions

| Agree | Discuss | Disagree |
|---|---|---|
| I think so too. | If you ask me, … | I don't think so. |
| I agree. | I don't know about that. | Sorry, but I disagree. |
| You're absolutely right. | That's true but … | You're completely wrong. |